Francis Spufford, a former *Sunday Times* ...

...thologies and a collection of essays about the history of technology. His first book, *I May Be Some Time*, won the Writers' Guild Award for Best Non-Fiction Book of 1996, the Banff Mountain Book Prize and a Somerset Maugham Award. His second, *The Child That Books Built*, gave Neil Gaiman 'the peculiar feeling that there was now a book I didn't need to write'. His third, *Backroom Boys*, was called 'as nearly perfect as makes no difference' by the *Daily Telegraph* and was shortlisted for the Aventis Prize. In 2007 he was elected a Fellow of the Royal Society of Literature. He teaches writing at Goldsmiths College and lives near Cambridge.

Further praise for *Unapologetic*:

'In a literary field that is fast becoming overpopulated, it is an intelligent, sophisticated and much welcome addition.' Nick Spencer, *New Statesman*

'An act of daring, a message from the frontline of an old and bruising war.' *Guardian*

'It comes as a relief not to be set by the author on the hamster wheel of Dawkins and anti-Dawkins arguments. Instead we are offered "a defence of Christian

emotions – their intelligibility and grown-up dignity."'
Christopher Howse, *Daily Telegraph*

'This wonderful book is one of the freshest writings about religion I've ever read . . . an encouraging and refreshing read for believers, reminding them of the sense faith can make . . . it also has the potential to move on the stale and stalled debate between atheism and Christianity in the West . . . I hope it comes into the hands of many unbelievers, not because it's above their criticism, but because it's worthy of it.' Stephen Tomkins, *Third Way* magazine

---

by the same author
I May Be Some Time
The Child that Books Built
Backroom Boys
Red Plenty

Unapologetic

FRANCIS SPUFFORD

ff

faber and faber

First published in this edition in 2012
by Faber and Faber Limited
Bloomsbury House,
74–77 Great Russell Street,
London WC1B 3DA

This paperback edition first published in 2013

Typeset by Faber and Faber Ltd

Printed and bound by CPI Group (UK) Ltd, Croydon, CR0 4YY

The right of Francis Spufford to be identified as author
of this work has been asserted in accordance with Section 77
of the Copyright, Designs and Patents Act 1988

A CIP record for this book
is available from the British Library

ISBN 978–0–571–22522–4

FSC
www.fsc.org
MIX
Paper from
responsible sources
FSC® C101712

2 4 6 8 10 9 7 5 3 1

For
Jessica
Judith
David
my three reverend doctors

1

Unapologetic

My daughter has just turned six. Some time over the next year or so, she will discover that her parents are *weird*. We're weird because we go to church.

This means – well, as she gets older there'll be voices telling her what it means, getting louder and louder until by the time she's a teenager they'll be shouting right in her ear. It means that we believe in a load of bronze-age absurdities. It means that we don't believe in dinosaurs. It means that we're dogmatic. That we're self-righteous. That we fetishise pain and suffering. That we advocate wishy-washy niceness. That we promise the oppressed pie in the sky when they die. That we're bleeding hearts who don't understand the wealth-creating powers of the market. That we're too stupid to understand the irrationality of our creeds. That we build absurdly complex intellectual structures, full of meaningless distinctions, on the marshmallow foundations of a fantasy. That we uphold the nuclear family, with all its micro-tyrannies and imprisoning stereotypes. That we're the hairshirted enemies of the ordinary family pleasures of parenthood, shopping, sex and car ownership. That we're savagely judgemental. That we'd free murderers to kill again. That we think everyone who disagrees with us is going to roast for all eternity. That we're as bad as Muslims. That we're worse than Muslims, because Muslims are primitives who can't be expected to know any better. That we're better than Muslims, but only because we've lost the courage of our convictions. That we're infantile and can't do without an illusory daddy in the sky. That we destroy the spontaneity and hopefulness of children by implanting a sick mythology in young minds. That we oppose freedom, human rights, gay rights, individual moral autonomy, a woman's right to choose, stem cell research, the use of condoms in fighting AIDS, the teaching of evolutionary biology. Modernity. Progress. That we think everyone should be cowering before authority. That we sanctify the idea of hierarchy. That we get all snooty and yuck-no-thanks about transsexuals, but think it's perfectly normal for middle-aged men to wear purple dresses. That we cover up child abuse, because we care more about power than justice. That we're the villains in history, on the wrong side of every struggle for human liberty. That if we sometimes seem to have been on the right side of one of said struggles, we weren't really; or the struggle wasn't about what it appeared to be about; or we didn't really do the right thing for the reasons we said we did. That we've provided pious cover stories for racism, imperialism, wars of conquest, slavery, exploitation. That we've manufactured imaginary causes for real people to kill each other. That we're stuck in the past. That we destroy tribal cultures. That we think the world's going to end. That we want to help the world to end. That we teach people to hate their own natural selves. That we want people to be afraid. That we want people to be ashamed. That we have an imaginary friend; that we believe in a sky pixie; that we prostrate ourseves before a god who has the reality status of Santa Claus. That we prefer scripture to novels, preaching to storytelling, certainty to doubt, faith to reason, law to mercy, primary colours to shades, censorship to debate, silence to eloquence, death to life.

But hey, that's not the bad news. Those are the objections of people who care enough about religion to object to it – or to rent a set of recreational objections from Richard Dawkins or Christopher Hitchens. As accusations, they may be a hodge-podge, a mish-mash of truths and half-truths and untruths plucked from radically different parts of Christian history and the Christian world, with the part continually taken for the whole (if the part is damaging) or the whole for the part (if it's flattering) – but at least they assume there's a thing called religion there which looms with enough definition and significance to be detested. In fact there's something truly devoted about the way that Dawkinsites manage to extract a stimulating hobby from the thought of other people's belief. The ones in this country must be envious of the intensity of the anti-religious struggle in the United States; yet some of them even contrive to feel oppressed by the Church of England, which is not easy to do. It must take a deft delicacy at operating on a tiny scale, like doing needlepoint, or playing Subbuteo, or fitting a whole model-railway layout into an attaché case.

No: the really painful message our daughter will

receive is that we're embarrassing. For most people who aren't New Atheists, or old atheists, and have no passion invested in the subject, either negative or positive, believers aren't weird because we're wicked. We're weird because we're inexplicable; because, when there's no necessity for it that anyone sensible can see, we've committed ourselves to a set of awkward and absurd attitudes which *obtrude*, which stick out against the background of modern life, and not in some important or respect-worthy or principled way either; more in the way that some particularly styleless piece of dressing does, which makes the onlooker wince and look away and wonder if some degree of cerebral deficiency is involved. Believers are people with pudding-bowl haircuts, wearing anoraks in August, and chunky-knit sweaters the colour of vomit. Or, to pull it back from the metaphor of clothing to the bits of behaviour that the judgement is really based on, believers are people who try to insert Jee-zus into conversations at parties; who put themselves down, with writhings of unease, for perfectly normal human behaviour; who are constantly trying to create a solemn hush that invites a fart, a hiccup, a bit of subversion. Believers are people who, on the rare occasions when you have to listen to them, like at a funeral or a wedding, seize the opportunity to pour the liquidised content of a primary-school nativity play into your earhole, apparently not noticing that childhood is over. And as well as being childish, and abject, and solemn, and awkward, we voluntarily associate ourselves with an old-fashioned mildewed orthodoxy, an Authority with all its authority gone. Nothing is so sad – sad from the style point of view – as the mainstream taste of the day before yesterday. If we couldn't help ourselves, if we absolutely had to go shopping in the general area of woo-hoo and The-Force-Is-Strong-In-You-Young-Skywalker, we could at least have picked something new and colourful, something with a bit of gap-year spiritual zing to it, possibly involving chanting and spa therapies. Instead of which, we chose old buildings that smell of dead flowers, and groups of pensioners laboriously grinding their way through 'All Things Bright and Beautiful'. Rebel cool? Not so much.

And worst, as I said before, *there is no reason for it.* No obvious lack that this sad stuff could be an attempt to supply, however cack-handed. Most people don't have a God-shaped space in their minds, waiting to be filled, or the New Atheist counterpart, a lack-of-God-shaped space, filled with the swirly, pungent vapours of polemic. Most people's lives provide them with a full range of loves and hates and joys and despairs, and a moral framework by which to understand them, and a place for awe and transcendence, without any need for religion. Believers are the people touting a solution without a problem, and an embarrassing solution too, a really damp-palmed, wide-smiling, can't-dance solution. In an anorak.

And so what goes on inside believers is mysterious. So far as it can be guessed at – if for some reason you *wanted* to guess at it – it appears to be a kind of anxious pretending, a kind of continual, nervous resistance to reality. It looks as if, to a believer, things can never be allowed just to be what they are. They always have to be translated, moralised – given an unnecessary and rather sentimental extra meaning. A sunset can't just be part of the mixed magnificence and cruelty and indifference of the world; it has to be a blessing. A meal has to be a present you're grateful for, even if it came from Tesco and the ingredients cost you £7.38. Sex can't be the spectrum of experiences you get used to as an adult, from occasional earthquake through to mild companionable buzz; it has to be, oh dear oh dear, a special thing that happens when mummies and daddies love each other very much. Presumably, all of these specific little refusals of common sense reflect our great big central failure of realism, our embarrassing trouble with the distinction, basic to adulthood, between stuff that exists and stuff that is made up. We don't seem to get it that the magic in *Harry Potter*, the rings and swords and elves in fantasy novels, the power-ups in video games, the ghouls and ghosts of Hallowe'en, are all, like, just for fun. We try to take them seriously; or rather, we take our own particular subsection of them seriously. We commit the bizarre category error of claiming that our goblins, ghouls, Flying Spaghetti Monsters are really there, off the page and away from the rendering programmes in the CGI studio. *Star Trek* fans and vampire wannabes have nothing on us. We actually get down and worship. We get down on our actual knees, bowing and scraping in front of the empty space where we insist our Spaghetti Monster can be found. No wonder that we work so hard to fend off common sense. Our fingers must be in our ears all the time – lalalala, I can't hear you – just to keep out the plain sound of the real world.

The funny thing is that to me it's exactly the other way around. In my experience, it's belief that involves the most uncompromising attention to the nature of things of which you are capable. It's belief which demands that you dispense with illusion after illusion, while contemporary common sense requires continual, fluffy pretending. Pretending that might as well be systematic, it's so thoroughly incentivised by our culture. Take the famous slogan on the atheist bus in London. I know, I know, that's an utterance by the hardcore hobbyists of unbelief, the people who care enough to be in a state of negative excitement about religion, but in this particular case they're pretty much stating the ordinary wisdom of everyday disbelief. (Rather than, for example, rabbiting on about orbital teapots.) The atheist bus says, 'There's probably no God. Now stop worrying and enjoy your life.' All right then: which word here is the questionable one, the aggressive one, the one that parts company with actual recognisable human experience so fast it doesn't even have time to wave goodbye? It isn't 'probably'. New Atheists aren't claiming anything outrageous when they say that there probably isn't a God. In fact they aren't claiming anything substantial at all, because really, how the fuck would they know? It's as much of a guess for them as it is for me. No, the word that offends against realism here is 'enjoy'. I'm sorry – *enjoy* your life? Enjoy your *life*? I'm not making some kind of neo-puritan objection to enjoyment. Enjoyment is lovely. Enjoyment is great. The more enjoyment the better. But enjoyment is *one emotion*. The only things in the world that are designed to elicit enjoyment and only enjoyment are products, and your life is not a product; you cannot expect to unwrap it, and place it in an advantageous corner of your Docklands flat, and admire the way the halogen spots on your lighting track gleam on its sleek sides. Only sometimes, when you're being lucky, will you stand in a relationship to what's happening to you where you'll gaze at it with warm, approving satisfaction. The rest of the time, you'll be busy feeling hope, boredom, curiosity, anxiety, irritation, fear, joy, bewilderment, hate, tenderness, despair, relief, exhaustion and the rest. It makes no more sense to say that you should feel the single emotion of enjoyment about your life than to say that you should spend it entirely in a state of fear, or of hopping-from-foot-to-foot anticipation. Life just isn't unanimous like that. To say that life is to be enjoyed (just enjoyed) is like saying that mountains should only have summits, or that all colours should be purple, or that all plays should be by Shakespeare. This really is a bizarre category error.

But not necessarily an innocent one. Not necessarily a piece of fluffy pretending that does no harm. The implication of the bus slogan is that enjoyment would be your natural state if you weren't being 'worried' by us believers and our hellfire preaching. Take away the malignant threat of God-talk, and you would revert to continuous pleasure, under cloudless skies. What's so wrong with this, apart from it being total bollocks? Well, in the first place, it buys a bill of goods, sight unseen, from modern marketing. Given that human life isn't and can't be made up of enjoyment, it is in effect accepting a picture of human life in which the pieces of living where easy enjoyment is more likely become the only pieces that are visible. You'd think, if you based your knowledge of the human species exclusively on adverts, that the normal condition of humanity was to be a good-looking single between twenty and thirty-five, with excellent muscle definition and/or an excellent figure, and a large disposable income. Clearly, there are exceptions, such as the lovey-dovey silver-agers who consume Viagra and go on Saga cruises, and the wisecracking moppets who promote breakfast cereal, but the centre of gravity of the human race, our default condition, is to be young, buff and available. And you'd think the same thing if you got your information exclusively from the atheist bus, with the minor difference that, in this case, the man from the Gold Blend couple has a tiny wrinkle of concern on his handsome forehead, caused by the troublesome thought of God's possible existence: a wrinkle about to be removed by one magic application of Reason™.

These plastic beings don't need anything that they can't get by going shopping. But suppose, as the atheist bus goes by, that you are the fifty-something woman

with the Tesco bags, trudging home to find out whether your dementing lover has smeared the walls of the
flat with her own shit again. Yesterday when she did
it, you hit her, and she mewled till her face was a mess
of tears and mucus which you also had to clean up.
The only thing that would ease the weight on your
heart would be to tell the funniest, sharpest-tongued
person you know about it: but that person no longer
inhabits the creature who will meet you when you un-
lock the door. Respite care would help, but nothing will
restore your sweetheart, your true love, your darling,
your jo. Or suppose you're that boy in the wheelchair,
the one with the spasming corkscrew limbs and the
funny-looking head. You've never been able to talk, but
one of your hands has been enough under your control to tap out messages. Now the electrical storm in
your nervous system is spreading there too, and your
fingers tap more errors than readable words. Soon
your narrow channel to the world will close altogether,
and you'll be left all alone in the hulk of your body. Research into the genetics of your disease may abolish it
altogether in later generations, but it won't rescue you.
Or suppose you're that skanky-looking woman in the
doorway, the one with the rat's nest of dreadlocks. Two
days ago you skedaddled from rehab. The first couple
of hits were great: your tolerance had gone right down,
over two weeks of abstinence and square meals, and
the rush of bliss was the way it used to be when you
began. But now you're back in the grind, and the news
is trickling through you that you've fucked up big time.

Always before you've had this story you tell yourself about getting clean, but now you see it isn't true, now you know you haven't the strength. Social services will be keeping your little boy. And in about half an hour you'll be giving someone a blowjob for a fiver behind the bus station. Better drugs policy might help, but it won't ease the need, and the shame over the need, and the need to wipe away the shame.

So when the atheist bus comes by, and tells you that there's probably no God so you should stop worrying and enjoy your life, the slogan is not just bitterly inappropriate in mood. What it means, if it's true, is that anyone who isn't enjoying themselves is entirely on their own. The three of you are, for instance; you're all three locked in your unshareable situations, banged up for good in cells no other human being can enter. What the atheist bus says is: there's no help coming. Now, don't get me wrong. I don't think there's any help coming, in one large and important sense of the term. I don't believe anything is going to happen which will materially alter the position these three people find themselves in. But let's be clear about the emotional logic of the bus's message. It amounts to a denial of hope or consolation, on any but the most chirpy, squeaky, bubble-gummy reading of the human situation. St Augustine called this kind of thing 'cruel optimism' fifteen hundred years ago, and it's still cruel.

Or for a piece of famous fluffiness that doesn't just pretend about what real lives can be like, but moves on into one of the world's least convincing pretences about what people themselves are like, consider the teased and coiffed nylon monument that is 'Imagine': surely the My Little Pony of philosophical statements. John and Yoko all in white, John at the white piano, John drifting through the white rooms of a white mansion, and all the while the sweet drivel flowing. Imagine there's no heaven. Imagine there's no hell. Imagine all the people, living life in – hello? Excuse me? Take religion out of the picture, and everybody spontaneously starts living life in *peace*? I don't know about you, but in my experience peace is not the default state of human beings, any more than having an apartment the size of Joey and Chandler's is. Peace is not the state of being we return to, like water running downhill, whenever there's nothing external to perturb us. Peace between people is an achievement, a state of affairs we put together effortfully in the face of competing interests, and primate dominance dynamics, and our evolved tendency to cease our sympathies at the boundaries of our tribe. Peace within people is made difficult to say the least by the way that we tend to have an actual, you know, emotional life going on, rather than an empty space between our ears with a shaft of dusty sunlight in it, and a lone moth flittering round and round. Peace is not the norm; peace is rare, and where we do manage to institutionalise it in a human society, it's usually because we've been intelligently pessimistic about human proclivities, and found a way to work with the grain of them in a system of intense mutual suspicion like the US Constitution, a document which assumes that absolutely everybody will be corrupt and power-hungry given half a chance. As for the inner version, I'm not at peace all that often, and I doubt you are either. I'm absolutely bloody certain that John Lennon wasn't. The mouthy Scouse git he was as well as the songwriter of genius, the leatherboy who allegedly kicked his best friend in the head in Hamburg, didn't go away just because he put on the white suit. What seems to be at work in 'Imagine' is the idea – always beloved by those who are frightened of themselves – that we're good underneath, good by nature, and only do bad things because we've been forced out of shape by some external force, some malevolent aspect of this world's power structures. In this case, I suppose, by the education the Christian Brothers were dishing out in 1950s Liverpool, which was strong on kicks and curses, and loving descriptions of the tortures of the damned. It's a theory that isn't falsifiable, because there always are power structures there to be blamed when people behave badly. Like the theory that markets left to themselves would produce perfectly just outcomes (when markets never are left to themselves) it's immune to disproof. But, and let me put this as gently as I can, it doesn't seem terribly likely. We long to believe it because it's what we lack. We dream of the peace we haven't got, and to make ourselves look as if we do have it, we dress ourselves up in the iconography of the heaven we just announced we were ditching. White robes, the celestial glare of over-exposed film: 'Imagine' looks like one part *A Matter of Life and Death* to one part *Hymns Ancient and Modern*. Only sillier.

A consolation you could believe in would be one that didn't have to be kept apart from awkward areas of reality. One that didn't depend on some more or less tacky fantasy about ourselves, and therefore one that wasn't in danger of popping like a soap bubble upon contact with the ordinary truths about us, whatever they turned out to be, good and bad and indifferent. A consolation you could trust would be one that acknowledged the difficult stuff rather than being in flight from it, and then found you grounds for hope in spite of it, or even because of it, with your fingers firmly out of your ears, and all the sounds of the complicated world rushing in, undenied.

I remember a morning about fifteen years ago. It was a particularly bad morning, after a particularly bad night. We had been caught in one of those cyclical rows that reignite every time you think they've come to an exhausted close, because the thing that's wrong won't be left alone, won't stay out of sight if you try to turn away from it. Over and over, between midnight and six, when we finally gave up and got up, we'd helplessly looped from tears, and the aftermath of tears, back into scratch-your-eyes-out scratch-each-other's-skin-off quarrelling, each time with the intensity undiminished, because the bitterness of the betrayal in question (mine) was not diminishing. Intimacy had turned toxic: we knew, as we went around and around and around it, almost exactly what the other one was going to say, and even what they were going to think, and it only made things worse. It felt as if we were reduced – but truth-fully reduced, reduced in accordance with the truth of the situation – to a pair of intermeshing routines, cogs with sharp teeth turning each other. When daylight came, the whole world seemed worn out. We got up, and she went to work. I went to a cafe – writer, you see, skivers the lot of us – and nursed my misery along with a cappuccino. I could not see any way out of sorrow that did not involve some obvious self-deception, some wishful lie about where we'd got to. (Where I'd got us to.) She wasn't opposite me any more, but I was still grinding round our night-long circuit in my head. And then the person serving in the cafe put on a cassette: Mozart's Clarinet Concerto, the middle movement, the Adagio.

If you don't know it, it is a very patient piece of music. It too goes round and round, in its way, es-sentially playing the same tune again and again, on the clarinet alone and then with the orchestra, clari-net and then orchestra, lifting up the same unhurried lilt of solitary sound, and then backing it with a kind of messageless tenderness in deep waves, when the strings join in. It is not strained in any way. It does not sound as if Mozart is doing something he can only just manage, and it does not sound as if the music is struggling to lift a weight it can only just manage. Yet at the same time, it is not music that denies anything. It offers a strong, absolutely calm rejoicing, but it does not pretend there is no sorrow. On the contrary, it sounds as if it comes from a world where sorrow is perfectly ordinary, but still there is more to be said. I had heard it lots of times, but this time it felt to me like news. It said: everything you fear is true. And yet. And yet. Everything you have done wrong, you have really done wrong. And yet. And yet. The world is wider than you fear it is, wider than the repeating rigmaroles in your mind, and it has *this* in it, as truly as it contains your unhappiness. Shut up and listen, and let yourself count, just a little bit, on a calm that you do not have to be able to make for yourself, because here it is, freely offered. You are still deceiving yourself, said the music, if you don't allow for the possibility of *this*. There is more going on here than what you deserve, or don't deserve. There is *this*, as well. And it played the tune again, with all the cares in the world.

The novelist Richard Powers has written that the Clarinet Concerto sounds the way mercy would sound, and that's exactly how I experienced it in 1997. 'Mercy', though, is one of those words that now requires definition. It does not only mean some tyrant's capacity to suspend a punishment he has himself inflicted. It can mean – and does mean in this case – getting something kind instead of the sensible consequences of an action, or as well as the sensible consequences of an action. Getting something kind where you thought there'd only be consequences. It isn't a question of some beetle-browed judge deciding not to punish you. It's just as much a question of something better than you could have expected being slipped, stealthily, into a process that was running anyway. Mercy is—

But by now I would imagine that some of you reading this are feeling some indignation building up. I
don't know who you are, of course, my dear particular
reader with this particular copy of the book in your
particular hands, or what you think about religion. You
may be an atheist with the light of combat in your eye,
or a fellow-believer hoping for a persuasive account of
what we share; you may be one of the large number of
non-believers who are mildly, tolerantly curious about
what faith can possibly feel like from the inside, in
what seems to you to be a self-evidently post-religious
world. Or you may fall into some different category altogether. I don't know, and I hope you'll excuse me if,
in my urgent desire to talk back at some of the loudest
and most frequent contemporary reactions to belief, I
seem to be shoving you, when I say 'you', into company
where you really don't belong. In this case by 'you' I
mean all of you who, as I start to wax eloquent about
mercy, are surging metaphorically to your feet with the
strong sensation that I just rushed past something important. ('Skating fast over thin ice', as Ralph Waldo
Emerson put it.)

Fair enough: if I get to interrupt Mr Lennon, you
certainly get to interrupt me. Wait a minute, wait a
minute, you say; never mind how you're defining
mercy. What about the way you're defining religion?
That's religion, listening to some Mozart in a cafe? You
were experiencing what we in the world of unbelief
like to call 'an emotion', an emotion induced by a form

of artistic expression which, to say the least, is quite famous for inducing emotions. You were not receiving a signal from God, or whatever it is you were about to claim; you were getting, if anything, a signal from Mr Mozart, that well-known dead Austrian in a wig. I hope that isn't your basis for religious faith, you say, because you've described nothing there that isn't compatible with a completely naturalistic account of the universe, in which there's *nobody there* to extend any magical mercy from the sky, just stuff, lots and lots of astonishing, sufficiently interesting stuff, all the way up from the quantum scale to the movement of galaxies.

Well, yes. By the same token, of course, what I've described is also completely compatible with a non-naturalistic account of the universe – but that's not really the point, is it? The point is that from outside, belief looks like a series of ideas about the nature of the universe for which a truth-claim is being made, a set of propositions that you sign up to; and when actual believers don't talk about their belief in this way, it looks like slipperiness, like a maddening evasion of the issue. If I say that, from inside, it makes much more sense to talk about belief as a characteristic set of feelings, or even as a habit, you will conclude that I am trying to wriggle out, or just possibly that I am not even interested in whether the crap I talk is true. I do, as a matter of fact, think that it is. For the record, I am not pulling the ultra-liberal, Anglican-going-on-atheist trick of saying that it's all a beautiful and interesting metaphor, snore bore yawn, and that religious terms mean whatever I want them to mean. (Though I do reserve the right to assert that believers get a slightly bigger say in what faith means than unbelievers do. It is *ours*, after all. Come in, if you think you're hard enough.) I am a fairly orthodox Christian. Every Sunday I say and do my best to mean the whole of the Creed, which *is* a series of propositions. No dancing about; no moving target, I promise. But it is still a mistake to suppose that it is assent to the propositions that makes you a believer. It is the feelings that are primary. I assent to the ideas because I have the feelings; I don't have the feelings because I've assented to the ideas.

So to me, what I felt listening to Mozart in 1997 is not some wishy-washy metaphor for an idea I believe in, and it's not a front behind which the real business of belief is going on: it's the thing itself. My belief is made of, built up from, sustained by, emotions like that. That's what makes it real. I do, of course, also have an interpretation of what happened to me in the cafe which is just as much a scaffolding of ideas as any theologian or Richard Dawkins could desire. I think – note the verb 'think' – that I was not being targeted with a timely rendition of the Clarinet Concerto by a deity who micromanages the cosmos and causes all the events in it to happen (which would make said deity an immoral scumbag, considering the nature of many of those events). I think that Mozart, two centuries earlier, had succeeded in creating a beautiful and accurate report of an aspect of reality. I think that the reason reality is that way, is in some ultimate sense merciful as well as being a set of physical processes all running along on their own without hope of appeal, all the way up from quantum mechanics to the relative velocity of galaxies by way of 'blundering, low and horridly cruel' biology (Darwin), is that the universe is sustained by a continual and infinitely patient act of love. I think that love keeps it in being. I think that Dante's cosmology was crap, but that he was right to say that it's 'love that moves the sun and all the other stars'.* I think that the universe is its own thing, integral, reliable, coherent, not Swiss-cheesed with irrationality or whimsical exceptions, and at the same time is never abandoned, not a single quark, proton, atom, molecule, cell, creature, continent, planet, star, cluster, galaxy, diverging metaversal timeline of it. I think that I don't have to posit some corny interventionist prod from a meddling sky fairy to account for my merciful ability to notice things a little better, when God is continually present everywhere anyway, undemonstratively underlying all cafes, all cassettes, all composers; when God is 'the ground of our being', as St Paul puts it, or as the Qur'an says with a slightly alarming anatomical specificity, when God 'is as close to you as the veins in your own neck'.

That's what I *think*. But it's all secondary. It all comes

---

* I've made a little alteration here. Dante actually said 'the sun and all the *lesser* stars', at the end of the *Paradiso*, because he was under the impression that the sun was a fire orbiting the earth, and the stars were a collection of much smaller sparkly objects stuck to the inner shell of a rotating crystal sphere. Like I said, his cosmology was crap.

limping along behind my emotional assurance that there was mercy, and I felt it. And so the argument about whether the ideas are true or not, which is the argument that people mostly expect to have about religion, is also secondary for me. No, I can't prove it. I don't know that any of it is true. I don't know if there's a God. (And neither do you, and neither does Professor Dawkins, and neither does anybody. It isn't the kind of thing you can know. It isn't a knowable item.) But then, like every human being, I am not in the habit of entertaining only the emotions I can prove. I'd be an unrecognisable oddity if I did. Emotions can certainly be misleading: they can fool you into believing stuff that is definitely, demonstrably untrue. But emotions are also our indispensable tool for navigating, for feeling our way through, the much larger domain of stuff that isn't susceptible to proof or disproof, that isn't checkable against the physical universe.[*] We dream, hope, wonder, sorrow, rage, grieve, delight, surmise, joke, detest; we form such unprovable conjectures as novels or clarinet concertos; we *imagine*. And religion is just a part of that, in one sense. It's just one form of imagining, absolutely functional, absolutely human-normal. It would seem perverse, on

---

[*] And isn't ever going to be, either, no matter the progress of science. Science is not ever, for example, going to provide us with the basis to make secure judgements about such works of human imagination as justice or mercy. For an excellent discussion of this point, see Richard Dawkins' explanation of his 'anti-Darwinian' political views in *A Devil's Chaplain*.

the face of it, to propose that this one particular manifestation of imagining should be treated as outrageous, should be excised if (which is doubtful) we can manage it.

But then, this is where the perception that religion is weird comes in. It's got itself established in our culture, relatively recently, that the emotions involved in religious belief must be different from the ones involved in all the other kinds of continuous imagining, hoping, dreaming, etc., that humans do. *These* emotions must be alien, freakish, sad, embarrassing, humiliating, immature, pathetic. *These* emotions must be quite separate from commonsensical us. But they aren't. The emotions that sustain religious belief are all, in fact, deeply ordinary and deeply recognisable to anybody who has ever made their way across the common ground of human experience as an adult. They are utterly familiar and utterly intelligible, and not only because the culture is still saturated with the spillage of Christianity, slopped out of the broken container of faith and soaked through everything. This is something more basic at work, an unmysterious consanguinity with the rest of experience.

It's just that the emotions in question aren't usually described in ordinary language, with no special vocabulary; aren't usually talked about apart from their rationalisation into ideas. That's what I shall do here. Ladies and gentlemen! A spectacle never before attempted on any stage! Before your very eyes, I shall build up from first principles the simple and unsurprising structure of faith. Nothing up my left sleeve, nothing up my right sleeve, except the entire material of everyday experience. No tricks, no traps, ladies and gentlemen; no misdirection and no cheap rhetoric. You can easily look up what Christians believe in. You can read any number of defences of Christian ideas. This, however, is a defence of Christian emotions – of their intelligibility, of their grown-up dignity. The book is called *Unapologetic* because it isn't giving an 'apologia', the technical term for a defence of the ideas.

And also because I'm not sorry.

2

The Crack in Everything

One of the major obstacles to communicating what belief feels like is that I'm not working with a blank slate. Our culture is smudged over with half-legible religious scribbling. The vocabulary that used to describe religious emotions hasn't gone away, or sunk into an obscurity from which you could carefully reintroduce it, giving a little explanation as each unfamiliar new/old term emerged. Instead, it's still in circulation, but repurposed, with new meanings generated by new usages; meanings that make people think that they know what believers are talking about when they really, really don't.

Case in point: the word 'sin', that well-known contemporary brand name for ice cream. And high-end chocolate truffles. And lingerie in which the colour red predominates. And sex toys; and cocktails. There's a brand-management agency in Australia called Sin. There's a fish restaurant in Lima, Peru, called Los Pescadores Capitales, which is a Spanish-language pun on the similarity between the words for sinning and for fishing. (An English equivalent would be The Seven Deadly Fins.) There used, God help us, to be a seaside panto for adults starring Jim Davidson which went by the name of *Sinderella*. Taxes on cigarettes and booze are 'sin taxes'. Sin City, in Frank Miller's comic book and the movie adaptation of it, is a locale where the population are entirely occupied in lap-dancing and extreme violence. Keep piling up the examples, and a picture emerges – meaning congealing from a pointillist cloud. It isn't tidy, this definition-by-use, and the cloud of meaning clearly has a light end (truffles) and a noir end (Frank Miller) but it's entirely comprehensible all the same.

'Sin', you can see, always refers to the pleasurable consumption of something. Also, it always preserves some connection to sex, which is why it would seem creepy for it ever to appear in the branding of a product aimed at children, and sometimes the sex is literal, but usually it's been disembodied, reduced to a mere tinge of the amosphere of desire, and transferred from sex itself to another bodily satisfaction, to eating or drinking or smoking or greedy looking (all of which are easier to put on sale in bulk quantities than sex itself). The other universal is that 'sin' always encodes a memory of ancient condemnation: but a distant memory, a very faint and inexplicable memory, just enough of a memory to add a zing of conscious naughtiness to whatever the pleasure in question is. Whether the thing you're consuming is saturated fat spiked with mood-lifting theobromine (truffles again) or the spectacle of non-existent impulse control rendered in moody black and white (Frank Miller again), you kind of know you shouldn't. But not in a serious way. The pleasure comes from committing an offence (against good nutrition or boring old good taste) which is too silly to worry about.

Everybody knows, then, that 'sin' basically means 'indulgence' or 'enjoyable naughtiness'. If you *were* worried, you'd use a different word or phrase. You'd talk about 'eating disorders' or 'addictions'; you'd go to another vocabulary cloud altogether. The result is that when you come across someone trying to use 'sin' in its old sense, you may know perfectly well in theory that they must mean something which isn't principally chocolatey, and yet the modern mood music of the word is so insistent that it's hard to hear anything except an invocation of a trivially naughty pleasure. And if someone talks, gravely and earnestly, about what a sorrowful burden one of those is, the result will be to make that speaker seem swiftly much, much more alarming than the thing they're getting worked up about. For which would seem to you to be the bigger problem, the bigger threat to human happiness: a plate of pralines, or a killjoy religious fanatic denouncing them?

If I say the word 'sin' to you, I'm basically buggered (as we like to say in the Church of England). It's going to sound as if I'm bizarrely opposed to pleasure, and because of the continuing link between 'sin' and sex, it will seem likely that at the root of my problem with pleasure is a problem with sex. You will diagnose me as a Christian body-hater. You'll corral me among the enemies of ordinary joy. You'll class me with the holy life-haters William Blake was thinking of, in the poem

26

in his *Songs of Experience* in which a chapel appears 'where I used to play on the green' –

> And tombstones where flowers should be:
> And Priests in black gowns were walking their
>   rounds,
> And binding with briars my joys and desires.

So I won't do that. Because that isn't at all what I mean. What I and most other believers understand by the word I'm not saying to you has got very little to do with yummy transgression. For us, it refers to something much more like the human tendency, the human propensity, to fuck up. Or let's add one more word: the human propensity to fuck *things* up, because what we're talking about here is not just our tendency to lurch and stumble and screw up by accident, our passive role as agents of entropy. It's our active inclination to break stuff, 'stuff' here including moods, promises, relationships we care about, and our own well-being and other people's, as well as material objects whose high gloss positively seems to invite a big fat scratch. Now, I hope, we're on common ground. In the end, almost everyone recognises this as one of the truths about themselves. You can get quite a long way through an adult life without having to acknowledge your own personal propensity to (etc. etc.); maybe even all the way through, if you're someone with a very high threshold of obliviousness, or with the kind of disposition that registers sunshine even

27

when a storm is howling all around. But for most of us the point eventually arrives when, at least for an hour or a day or a season, we find we have to take notice of our HPtFtU (as I think I'd better call it). Our appointment with realisation often comes at one of the classic moments of adult failure: when a marriage ends, when a career stalls or crumbles, when a relationship fades away with a child seen only on Saturdays, when the supposedly recreational coke habit turns out to be exercising veto powers over every other hope and dream. It need not be dramatic, though. It can equally well just be the drifting into place of one more pleasant, indistinguishable little atom of wasted time, one more morning like all the others, which quietly discloses you to yourself. You're lying in the bath and you notice that you're thirty-nine and that the way you're living bears scarcely any resemblance to what you think you've always wanted; yet you got here by choice, by a long series of choices for things which, at any one moment, temporarily outbid the things you say you wanted most. And as the water cools, and the light of Saturday morning in summer ripples heartlessly on the bathroom ceiling, you glimpse an unflattering vision of yourself as a being whose wants make no sense, don't harmonise: whose desires, deep down, are discordantly arranged, so that you truly want to possess and you truly want not to, at the very same time. You're equipped, you realise, for farce (or even tragedy) more than you are for happy endings. The HPtFtU dawns on you. You have, indeed, fucked things up. Of course you have. You're human, and that's where we live; that's our normal experience.

(Which is the reason, by the way, that I've started the tour of religion's recognisable emotions here, with this undeniably gloomy shit. I could, after all, have put us on the traditional night-time hilltop, and had us gaze out at stars more numerous than the sand grains on a beach, and the red-shifted exhaust of galaxies revving away from us. I could have put our hearts in our mouths and filled us with awe at the bigness of it all; with the luminous, numinous Carl-Sagan-osity of things, which even Richard Dawkins agrees ought to stir us to our depths, though what it should stir us to *do*, of course, is to seek out a career in the empirical sciences. I will give awe its due later, I promise, but the trouble with it as a starting-point is that it is, by its nature, a rather isolated emotion, marked out by its sudden self-forgetting focus on an object external to us, and by its disconnection from everyday trundling along. If awe is powerful, it tends to be a state we fall out of knackered, after a while, unable to keep up the intensity. If it's more modest, it tends of its nature to fade away anyway, to peter out on the hilltop where it began. And in neither case is it obvious how awe is supposed to relate to the rest of experience. I think of awe as a kind of National Trust property among feelings: somewhere to visit from time to time, but not a place you can live.)

The HPtFtU is bad news, and like all bad news is not very welcome, especially if you let yourself take seriously the implication that we actually *want* the destructive things we do, that they are not just an accident that keeps happening to poor little us, but part of our nature; that we are truly cruel as well as truly tender, truly loving and at the same time truly likely to take a quick nasty little pleasure in wasting or breaking love, scorching it knowingly up as the fuel for some hotter or more exciting feeling. We would, on the whole, very much like this not to be true, and our culture conspires to help us avoid and defer and ignore the sting of it as much as possible. The purveyors of flattering images do their damnedest to keep us feeling that we can be as we wish ourselves to be. It would not be very cool or aspirational if we had to imagine our biographies being sculpted out of some awkward substance over which we had limited control. In the ideal land of marketing, you can choose what you are. Each minute is supposed to be the solvent of the one before. All that is solid is supposed to melt into air. If you do get upset about some aspect of your own actions, the advice you get is not to dwell on it; to banish it, in effect, by applying a sense of proportion. Think of all the good stuff that's also true about you! Well, yes: yet seeing your virtues clearly is difficult for exactly the same reasons that seeing your HPtFtU is, so the advice amounts to a suggestion, really, that you should distract yourself. Keep yourself busy with stuff. Don't look inside. Shop. Rent a DVD. Kill some zombies on your Xbox. Let the net's unending flutter of opinions tickle you, and keep you tickled.

When our desires do conflict sharply enough to cause us an unhappiness we can't distract away, there is a strong contemporary feeling that it ought to be possible to fix the situation by a change in the rules, an alteration of what is and is not permissible. We've been telling ourselves a very popular story recently, about a person poisoned by anxiety and self-hatred because they think they are forbidden to do something essential to their nature; then they discover that the prohibition is groundless, that it's a meaningless taboo left over from less enlightened times which they could and should discard. And so they do the thing they've wanted and feared to do – they go to bed with someone of their own gender, they leave the violent husband who belittles them, they explore the polyamorous lifestyle – and it's OK. The sky doesn't fall. The ground is still solid under their feet. And they relax into freedom. Think of Stephen Fry in *Wilde*, when he's lying next to another man for the first time, saying 'I feel like a city that's been under siege for years, and suddenly the gates are thrown open . . .' This is a potent contemporary myth, and like all potent myths, it has a large amount of truth in it. Over the last fifty years, we really have been escaping, as a culture, from a set of cruel and constricting rules, particularly about sexuality and gender roles, which (yes) did have the sanction of religion behind them. (Not that religion *caused* those rules to exist, on the whole. There was a malignant cultural consensus in place in their favour, of which religion was a part.) But the truth that some problems of conflicted desire can be solved this way, some cases in which we desperately both want and don't want to do something, doesn't mean it's true that all can. Any more than the possibility of abolishing particular rules of behaviour means that we could plausibly abolish all rules of behaviour. There's always, necessarily, going to be stuff it's all right to do and stuff it's emphatically not all right to do. We discover new immoralities to take seriously at the same speed that we abolish old ones. Just as much as our ancestors, but about different things, we're sure that people are *rightly* horrified if they find they have certain feelings. Make the thought experiment of turning the man who wants and doesn't want to want sex with other men into a man who wants and doesn't want to want sex with children: immediately our feeling vanishes that it's the existence of a prohibition which is the problem. And no, I'm not saying that those two desires are in any way morally equivalent. I'm saying that soluble problems of conflicted desire represent a lucky subset of a much larger class of insoluble ones, states of tangled wanting we aren't going to reform away. There can never *not* be a situation in which people will find it essential to be a certain way, will want and need to be a certain way, and find that they cannot manage it. We are creatures who don't get to decide what we are, whose natures are always partly hidden from our conscious understanding, who always pull several ways at once. It's an insight that can be restated in radically different analytical terms, and still have the same implications for experience.

You can put it as Freud did, and say that there are unconscious processes which resist and subvert conscious intentions. You can think of it in terms of evolutionary biology, in which case one of the best expressions of it is the geneticist Bill Hamilton's wonderful description of the human animal as 'an ambassador sent forth by an unstable coalition'. Or you can quote St Paul: 'What I would not, that I do. What I would, that I do not.' Wherever the line is drawn between good and evil, between acceptable and unacceptable, between kind and cruel, between clean and dirty, we're always going to be voting on both sides of it, despite ourselves. Not all of us, on every subject, all the time, of course; but all of us on some subject or other some of the time.

And this is a state of affairs in the face of which we are, for the most part, currently clueless, toolless, committed to alarmed denial rather than to any more useful or hopeful response. It's not that we aren't *interested* in evil, as a culture. We are, terribly, especially when it manifests itself in sensational and extreme forms. Think of the rise and rise, and rise and rise, and further rise, of the serial-killer romance since Thomas Harris invented it in its modern form with *The Silence of the Lambs*, and its diversification into torture porn. There are now far more fictional serial killers operating than there have ever been of the very rare kind of real murderer who preys on strangers. But then the function of the serial killer, as a modern mythological figure, is to concentrate an anxiety which is very widely shared, almost universal even – our anxiety about living among strangers, about being alarmingly reliant on the behaviour of the unknowns we move among every day. The serial-killer story finds a way to acknowledge that human behaviour is a continuum, a distribution under a normal curve maybe, with some very odd things at the ends of it, from which we are not insulated except by chance and probability, if we live in a big enough city, in a connected enough network, in a world wide enough to accommodate the spread of what people do. Out there at those ends – we keep being reminded – out there at the tail of human probability, there are terrors, which the serial-killer story renders with don't-look-away gross-out literalism, as people who want to have at us with surgical instruments or chainsaws or a knife and fork. When it comes to anyone who might want to skin us in a cellar, we're quite happy to agree that 'evil' is the appropriate term. (Which is one reason why the genre is an unexpected redoubt of traditional moral schemes, albeit often treated ironically, or as a cause of horror in themselves. If you want the seven deadly sins taken as something other than food-styling cues, go to David Fincher's *Seven*.) The rather severe limitation on the way the serial-killer story does evil, though, is that it always offers it to us as, exactly, something out there, something far distant from us, which by bad luck descends growling and licking its lips on ordinary old, innocent old us, who live in the nice normal middle of the normal curve. It is the predator, we are the prey. It is the doer of the harm. We are the done unto. Which is superficially scary, and then very, very cosy.

But HPtFtU is in here, not out there. The bad news is bad news about us, not just about other people. And when the conviction of it settles in, when we reach one of those stages of our lives where the sorrow of our failure hangs in our chests like a weight, and waking up in the morning is painful because every time the memory of what's wrong has to ooze back over the lovely blankness of the night – you'll know what I mean if you've ever been there – then, the idea that it would help to cling to a cosy sense of victimhood seems as silly as it would be to try and fight off the flu by waving a toy lightsaber. The bad news, at those moments, feels like the whole truth about you. It isn't. It is only *a* truth about you. But the way back to the rediscovery of the rest of what's true begins with the admission that you really are guilty of the particular bit of HPtFtU whch is making you feel like shit. If you don't give the weight in your chest its true name you can't even begin. It's guilt that drags at your steps, it's guilt that paints the morning black. In my experience, in times of intense misery it's letting your guilt be guilt that at least stops you needing to accuse yourself; and in better times, in times of more or less cheerful ordinary muddling through, I've found that admitting there's some black in the colour-chart of my psyche doesn't invite the blot of dark to swell, or give a partial truth more gloomy power over me than it should have, but the opposite. Admitting there's some black in the mixture makes it matter less. It makes it easier to pay attention to the mixedness of the rest. It helps you stop wasting your time on denial, and therefore helps you stop ricocheting between unrealistic self-praise and unrealistic self-blame. It helps you be kind to yourself.

'Guilt', though, gets a terrible press now: much worse than frothy, frivolous 'sin'. Our culture *does* take it seriously, but as a cause of unhappiness in itself, a wanton anxiety-generator. It's as if the word 'groundless' always slid invisibly into place in our sentences next to it. As if it were always a false signal, a fuss being made about nothing by somebody who shouldn't be beating themselves up over playing tiddly-winks on the Sabbath. Once again, our usage assumes a world where we never do anything it would be appropriate to feel bad about. So the old expressions of guilt stop sounding like functional responses to real situations and become evidence of crazy self-hatred. Strike up the New Orleans big band, please:

> Amazing grace, how sweet the sound
> That saved a wretch like me . . .

There! Did you hear that? He just called himself a wretch. He's beating himself up in public. Sorry, mate: lovely tune, loony sentiment. Except that 'wretch' is actually a very polite word for what John Newton, the eighteenth-century author of 'Amazing Grace', was. John Newton was a slave trader. He made his living transporting cargoes of kidnapped human beings, in conditions of great squalor and suffering, to places where they and their children and their children's children would be treated all their lives as objects to be bought and sold and brutalised. Some of John Newton's contemporaries (the ones who weren't chained below decks in their own shit) may have thought that his profession was only a bit unrespectable; we, on the other hand, recognise that he was participating in one of the world's great crimes, comparable to the Holocaust. Wretch? John Newton was a horror.

But at least he came to know it. At least he made the journey from comfortable acquiescence in horror to an accurate, and therefore horrified, sense of himself. At least he learned that something was wrong. And 'Amazing Grace' is a description of the process by which he began to awaken. The wrinkle is that he wrote it *before* he gave up slaving. He wrote it under the impression that he had *already* seen the stuff he should be worrying about – booze and licentiousness, presumably, and playing tiddly-winks on the Sabbath, and not running his slave ship with a swear-box screwed to the mast. In the Holocaust analogy, it's rather as if a death-camp guard had had a moral crisis, but over cheating his colleagues at poker, and then continued to come to work stoking the ovens, while vowing shakily to be a better person. Yet Newton's guilt, once found, wouldn't leave him alone. It went on gradually showing him dark, accurate visions of himself; it went on changing him, until eventually he could not bear the darkness of what he did daily, and gave up the trade, and ended his life as a penitent campaigner against it. At every stage, it had been the same patient guilt that led him on, and so 'Amazing Grace', which records its earliest gnawing at him, is unwittingly faithful to the rest of what was coming to him. "Twas grace that taught my heart to fear', he says in the second verse, and what he's reporting there is his feeling, his *amazed* feeling, which we probably wouldn't want to disagree with under the circumstances, that he'd been done a massive undeserved favour by being allowed to become frightened of himself. The night sweats, the uncontrollable memories, the waking to misery, were all in his case a gift, a lucky bounty he couldn't ever have earned. (We'll get to definitions of 'grace' later.) There are some human states to which guilty fear is the absolutely appropriate response; on which guilty fear is an immense improvement; from which guilty fear is the first step of the only available rescue. 'Amazing Grace' has been popular for two and a half centuries – has been claimed by millions of hearers and singers as true to their own experience – because it has been, so to speak, tested (unwittingly) at the extremes of what human beings ought to feel guilty about. If there's room for John Newton to make peace with his terrifying variety of HPtFtU, there's room for everyone.

I'd argue that guilt is also a perfectly functional and appropriate emotion in much milder cases. In fact, I'd argue that guilt is often an instrument of self-discovery, telling you a new thing about parts of yourself which other people may have praised to the skies

– and praised *rightly*. Take the very bad night experienced in February 1976, not long before he died, by the eighty-eight-year-old Field Marshal Montgomery. His housekeeper, alarmed, rang an old friend who had been one of his battalion commanders, and when the friend came over and asked what the matter was, Montgomery said, 'I've got to go to meet God, and explain all those men I killed at Alamein.' Now, please push to one side for the moment the questions of whether there is a God, and whether dead people go to meet him, and concentrate instead on the source of the general's disquiet. It was being generated by his biography, not by his theology. Remarkably, it was a piece of guilt arising on the ground of one of his great military virtues.

Montgomery had had flaws all right, as a general. He was monstrously vain, he antagonised almost everyone he ever had to deal with as an equal, and sometimes his plans miscarried spectacularly, as at Arnhem. But he didn't, ever, waste his soldiers' lives. When it came to killing the enemy he was naturally less scrupulous, but even there he was immune to the Napoleonic, or Hitlerian, or Stalinesque fondness for grandiose bloodletting. He was a spectacularly good general for a democracy having an emergency, because he knew how to turn heterogeneous conscripted citizens into effective components of an army, and then, having done that, went on treating them as precious and valuable. He knew this about himself; he was proud of it; and until this very late moment in his life, he had been morally comfortable with himself as a result. At the second battle of El Alamein in October–November 1942, his strategy had been as frugal as the situation allowed. The Eighth Army, to whose command he had just been promoted, was only half-trained by his standards and could not yet be counted on for a battle of manoeuvre, which, in any case, was what the opposing Afrika Korps excelled at. So, since he had the superiority in troops and armour, he settled on a battle of attrition, with his own soldiers advancing through minefields to engage the enemy within their defensive positions. He did not waste lives, but he spent them. His victory cost 13,500 casualties (dead and wounded combined) among 220,000 Allied soldiers on the battlefield. Alamein was bloody, but it was parsimoniously bloody compared to the all-hours slaughterhouse operating at Stalingrad at the same time, or to any of the frontal assaults masterminded by British generals in the trenches of the First World War, where Montgomery had been as a young officer. Above all, his strategy *worked*. The lives he sacrificed, he sacrificed to a purpose.

So what had he noticed now that he should feel guilty about? Nothing could be more presumptuous than speculating about other people's consciences, but I'll do it anyway. My guess would be that he had started thinking, in the small hours of his bad night, about the individual fates of the individual bodies of those he had sent forward through the mines, and about how little the purposefulness of the advance must have helped, when the sand suddenly heaved up from beneath and an expanding ball of force tore away legs, arms, eyes, faces. My guess would be, in other words, that though the necessities of the battle remained the same, he had stopped seeing necessity as a complete justification. He had noticed that no matter how few soldiers his strategy killed, and no matter how many more would have been killed if a less careful strategist had been in charge, and no matter how essential it was that *somebody* be in charge – nevertheless, the deaths he caused had been absolute in their significance for those who had done the dying. Generals have to think statistically, judging four deaths to be better than five, but people don't die statistically, they die in ones, and for each person the loss is complete and incomparable. It is the erasure of the entire sum of things, the obliteration of the whole world. It doesn't make it better to know that your death is part of a smaller statistic.

Beyond the technical skills of generalship, and the ethics of generalship, there was this other consideration. Beyond the truth that war organises murders to serve the greater good, there was the truth that the murders were still murder. You could do what must be done, and do it as well as possible, and it would still be the case that locally, body by body, the consequences were cruel and sad, and left the fabric of the world tattered and bloodstreaked where an individual postman failed to go home to Carmarthen, or a tall schoolteacher was wept over in Adelaide. I think Bernard Montgomery was frightened, in February 1976, because he had understood that even necessary actions could contribute to the miserable sum of HPtFtU. I also think that (if I'm right in my presumptuous guess) his fear was very much to his credit. He had made a real discovery in finding this new thing to worry about, at the very end of his life. His fear, that night, was a sign of something in him growing, at almost the last possible moment: an old brown general putting out a fresh green shoot. His biography doesn't record what his friend said to him in return. We just have to hope that it reassured him.

Suppose, though, that the friend had tried to ease his fear by telling him he was imagining things. Would that have helped? No, surely not. If you tell somebody that, as a decent person, they cannot have done anything questionable, you may mean to be nice, but you are in reality denying them sympathy. You are refusing to go to them where they are, you are declining to join them in the emotion they are finding painful. Somebody who is accusing herself or himself of something may well be mistaken, factually or morally, in that particular instance; but not because they are incapable of wrongdoing. No one is incapable of wrongdoing, and we have to be allowed our capacity for HPtFtU if we are to have our full stature. Taking the things people do wrong seriously is part of taking *them* seriously. It's part of letting their actions have weight. It's part of letting their actions *be* actions rather than just indifferent shopping choices; of letting their lives tell a life-story, with consequences, and losses, and gains, rather than just being a flurry of events. It's part of letting them be real enough to be worth loving, rather than just attractive or glamorous or pretty or charismatic or cool.

But this is difficult and uncomfortable, unless someone has done something so spectacularly repulsive that they can be safely banished to the separated domain of wickedness where the serial killers and the child molesters champ and dribble. We find it hard to acknowledge the seriousness of ordinary screw-ups, because we get very worried by the idea that we might be judging people, 'judgemental' being another Bad Word of our time – or 'sitting in judgement' on them, which draws the instant mental picture of us being raised above them, on some kind of courtroom throne, gazing down with a brow like thunder. And isn't this what religion famously encourages people to do? To judge, to criticise, to carp, to find fault? Well, no. (Though lots of religious people do carp, criticise, judge, find fault. See above, under: HPtFtU. I may, ahem, be a little inclined to fault-finding myself.) Ironically enough, the taboo about being 'judgemental' wasn't formed in our culture in reaction to religion; it isn't part of the great journey into the secular light on which A. C. Grayling is leading us, tossing his miraculously bouffant locks. It is, itself, a little piece of inherited Christianity, a specifically Christian prohibition which has turned proverbial and floated free of its context, origins all forgotten, until we imagine that it means we shouldn't even think in terms of good and bad. Originally, what it meant was that we shouldn't think of good and bad in terms of laws, or in terms of a courtroom procedure which would find people guilty or not guilty.

In fact, this is the crucial* point at which Christianity parts company with the other two monotheisms. Unlike the oldest (Judaism) and the youngest (Islam) of the one-god religions, the middle sibling isn't interested in coming up with a set of sustainable rules for living by. Jewish laws of behaviour and Muslim laws of behaviour may be demanding to keep at times, but they can be kept. That's the point of them, that's what they're for. Eating kosher or halal can involve juggling with saucepans and reading the sides of packets carefully, but it isn't privation. Getting up for the dawn prayer can be a pain, but it won't leave you short of sleep, if you go to bed at a sensible hour. Refraining from work on Shabbat is tricky, if you define 'work' to include all household chores, and it takes some organisation, but not an impossible degree of organisation. Wiggle-room is kindly built in to the rules, so that you can cope if your water main bursts on Shabbat, or if you're travelling and there really is no way of telling the direction to pray in. Nothing crazy or superhuman is required of you. The idea is to have a set of laws like a wearable coat, a coat that everyone can put on if they are willing to make the effort. In Judaism and Islam, you don't have to be a saint to know that you are managing to

---

* Pun intended. Sorry.

be an adequately good woman, an adequately good man. Islam and Judaism accomplish this livability, this wearability, this sustainability, by paying more attention to what people do than to what they feel about it. They're religions of orthopraxy, right doing, not orthodoxy, right thinking or teaching. Do the right actions, and you can be hissing and spitting inside, or bored senseless, or going through the motions to please your family, and it still counts. Virtue has still been achieved. The result is in some ways a lot more moderate, a lot more stable than Christianity; and it can be very humane too, with plentiful opportunities for the unvirtuous or ex-virtuous to rejoin virtue's ranks. But it does, indeed, produce a judged picture of the world. It produces a moralised landscape in which the good people can be told from the bad people; in which all human actions can be split into two categories, pure or impure, clean or dirty, permitted or forbidden, kosher or trayf, halal or haram.

Christianity does something different. It makes frankly impossible demands. Instead of asking for specific actions, it offers general but lunatic principles. It thinks you should give your possessions away, refuse to defend yourself, love strangers as much as your family, behave as if there's no tomorrow. These principles do not amount to a sustainable programme. They deliberately ignore the question of how they could possibly be maintained. They ask you to manifest in your ordinary life a drastically uncalculating, unprotected generosity. And that's not all. Christianity also makes what you

mean by your behaviour all-important. You could pau-
perise yourself, get slapped silly without fighting back,
care for lepers and laugh all day long in the face of fu-
tures markets, and it still wouldn't count, if you did it
for the wrong reasons. Not only is Christianity insanely
perfectionist in its few positive recommendations, it's
also insanely perfectionist about motive. It won't accept
generosity performed for the sake of self-interest *as*
generosity. It says that unless altruism is altuism all the
way down, it doesn't count as altruism at all.

So far, so thrillingly impractical. But now notice the
consequence of having an ideal of behaviour not sized
for human lives: everyone fails. Really *everyone*. No one
only means well, no one means well all the time. Looked
at from this perspective, human beings all exhibit different varieties of fuck-up. And suddenly in its utter
lack of realism Christianity becomes very realistic indeed, intelligently resigned to our vast array of imper-
fections, and much more interested in what we can do
to live with them than in laws designed to keep them
segregated. Christianity maintains no register of clean
and unclean. It doesn't believe in the possibility of
clean, just as it doesn't believe that laws can ever be fully
adequate, or that goodness can reliably be achieved by
following an instruction book. The moral landscape
Christianity sees – well, it's essentially as described by
Leonard Cohen. All due apologies offered to Mr
Golden Voice, who I'm sure thought he was satirising
religion in 'Anthem', and offering an atheistical Jewish
Buddhist's alternative to sanctimonious certainty. But

instead 'Anthem' works, if you're a Christian, as sympathetic reportage of our rueful orthodoxies. We do try to ring the bells that still can ring, though much of the carillon is corroded, or lost to metal fatigue, or otherwise spoiled. We do forget our perfect offering – tell ourselves to forget it, since perfection is forever unavailable. We do entirely agree that there's a crack in everything. (That's how the light gets in? Oh yes; that most of all.) The vision is of an intrinsically imperfect cosmos, hairlined through and through with flaws, chipped and battered and patched.

So of all things, Christianity *isn't* supposed to be about gathering up the good people (shiny! happy! squeaky clean!) and excluding the bad people (frightening! alien! repulsive!) for the very simple reason that there aren't any good people. Not that can be securely designated as such. It can't be about circling the wagons of virtue out in the suburbs and keeping the unruly inner city at bay. This, I realise, goes flat contrary to the present predominant image of it as something existing in prissy, fastidious little enclaves, far from life's messier zones and inclined to get all 'judgemental' about them. Again, of course there are Christians like that: see under HPtFtU. The religion certainly can slip into being a club or a cosy affinity group or a wall against the world. But it isn't supposed to be. What it's supposed to be is a league of the guilty. Not all guilty of the same things, or in the same way, or to the same degree, but enough for us to recognise each other. For

HPtFtU, after all, isn't a list of prohibited actions you can avoid.* Fucking things up is too sensitive to our intentions to be defined that way. The very same action may be a secret kindness, an indifferent bit of trivia, or a royally destructive contribution to the ruination of something delicate and precious, all depending on what we mean by it. (There are remarks that end marriages, and very often what makes them so decisively poisonous is that they're chosen to seem perfectly innocent and ordinary when uttered in public, no big deal, deniable, yet touch deliberately on a pain which only intimacy could know.) What we have to rely on, to tell whether something is part of HPtFtU or not, is more like a family resemblance. We define it by our familiarity with examples, we name it as what the examples have in common, as if we were defining 'yellowness' as the thing that a JCB shares with a mustard pot. In the same way, we come to see, HPtFtU is what flying a plane into a skyscraper has in common with persecuting the fat kid with zits. It's what doing crystal meth has in common with having an affair with someone you don't even like. It's what a murder (not a pop-culture play murder but a real murder, committed by delivering one too many kicks to the head in a pissed fight at closing time) has in common with telling a story at a dinner party

---

* Even the neatly-arranged Seven Deadlies, product of medieval Christianity at its most legalistic, couldn't be exhaustive, or be used as more than a field guide to some of HPtFtU's major varieties.

at the expense of an absent mutual friend, a story which you know will cause pain when it gets back to them but which you tell anyway, because it's just very, very funny. Little, large, venial, deadly, in hot blood or in cold blood, done actively or allowed to happen through negligence – there's a look the instances of HPtFtU have in common, elusive to summarise but unmistakeable when seen: a certain self-pleasing smirk. Christianity wants us to know the look when we see it in a mirror, and to know it too when we see it reflected in other people. Christians are supposed to understand that the family resemblance makes us family even with the nastiest and most frightening of our brothers and sisters: a different kind of continuum. We're supposed to do our fallible, failing best to perceive the other bad people as kin.

Which all sounds, oh, a little too resolved. A little too neat. Not neat in the sense that a ranked gradation of the world by virtue would be, but neat in the sense that I've fast-forwarded, here, through the pain of self-discovery and the discomfort of mutual recognition to get to the equanimity that can lie on the other side. It really can; there really is a rueful, unanguished comfort to be had over there, through and beyond. But I've got way ahead of myself. First you have to go through; and while you do, while you're struggling with the first raw realisation of the degree to which you've fucked (things) up, in one of the louder or quieter crises of adult life, there is no resolution to be had, no comfy scheme of order to hold on to. The essence of the experience I'm trying to talk about in this chapter is that it's chaotic. You stop making sense to yourself. You find that you aren't what you thought you were, but something much more multiple and mysterious and self-subverting, and this discovery doesn't propel you to a new understanding of things, it propels you into a state where you don't understand anything at all. Unable to believe the comfortable things you used to believe about yourself, you entertain a sequence of changing caricatures as your self-image. By turns your reflection in the mirror of your imagination nonsensically grins, scowls, howls, yawns, gazes back inert as a lump of putty: decomposes into pixels that have forgotten the reason for their mutual attachment. Here is a description of the state from a Hebrew poem 2,600 years old: 'I am poured out like water, and all my bones are out of joint; my heart is like wax; it is melted in the midst of my bowels.' And here is a description by John Bunyan in the 1660s: 'Thus did I wind, and twine, and shrink, under the burden that was upon me; which burden also did so oppress me that I could neither stand, nor go, nor lie, either at rest or quiet.' And here is a description by the psychologist William James in 1902: 'The normal process of life contains moments as bad as any of those which insane melancholy is filled with, moments in which radical evil gets its innings and takes its solid turn.'

And here is a description by Marilynne Robinson, in a novel of 2008:

Della's father . . . told me I was nothing but trouble. I felt the truth of that. I really am nothing . . . Nothing, with a body. I create a kind of displacement around myself as I pass through the world, which can fairly be called trouble. This is a mystery, I believe . . . It's why I keep to myself. When I can.

It doesn't change much, chaos. I'm running a risk here, that you as you read this will fail to recognise a condition I'm putting a lot of explanatory stress on as a human universal, and I'm sure that there is a lot of variation between temperaments: but I don't think there are many adults to whom this has never happened at all. If you don't recognise it in the slightest, then I submit that either (a) you aren't paying attention, or (b) you are very, very lucky.

I want to give chaos its due here, unmodified, unconsoled, not yet smoothed into a new status quo; rough as it is the first night after you move out of the marital home. Because it is in that chaos, that true realisation of a true formlessness in yourself, that the need can begin which is one of the strong motives for belief, one of the basic emotions from which the rest unfolds. It's only one of them. Certainly there are others, other strong needs that serve as starting-points: for comfort in sorrow, for company in isolation, for guidance in perplexity. They aren't all negative, either. People can and do begin sometimes with a state of powerful happiness, one that blows in like weather and yet feels so substantial that they learn it can be leant on, depended on, built on. And I'll grudgingly agree that now and then awe – all right, all right – need not be a *total* National Trust property, at which we only have visitors' rights. Now and again, permanent things can result from being transfixed, struck into wonder by some powerful displacement of our ordinary awareness. But it's the guilty chaos of HPtFtU that I'll follow, since so much in Christian belief particularly follows from it.

For what do we *do* with the knowledge that we've fucked up, that we no longer make sense to ourselves? Turn to face each other, for a start. A community of acknowledged fuck-ups ought at least in theory to be kinder to one another. And there are things we can use our imperfection for, once we admit it: structures that can be built from unreliable parts and yet be reliable themselves, like the constitutional order of the American republic, or the scientific method, or the internet. But there's a limit to what we can do for each other, a limit to how much of each other's HPtFtU we can ever manage to bear – even just to bear to *hear* about – while it often feels as if there's no limit to how far or how long the ripples of our multitudinous fuck-ups can keep travelling, or how intricately they can go on colliding and encroaching and causing collateral damage in other lives. Think of the consequences of John Newton's HPtFtU, still fresh and vigorous after two hundred years. In this case, and in plenty of others where the harm is ongoing, it wouldn't even be right to ask for help with the aftermath of doing the harm.

Should John Newton's victims have been asked to make him feel better about what he'd done to them? I think not. We have to attend to justice as well as mercy, and we're finite creatures, with limited powers to make good what's been broken. With the best will in the world, we can't always take the weight of other people's bad stuff, we can't often lean in and lift it off them. The crack in everything is here to stay.

So one thing we do instead, when we've fucked up, when we no longer make sense to ourselves, is to turn towards the space where the possibility exists that there might be someone to hear us who is not one of the parties to our endless, million-sided, multigenerational suit against each other. To turn towards a space in which there is quite possibly no one – in which, we think as we find ourselves doing it, that there probably *is* no one.

And we say: Hello? Hello? I don't think I can stand this any more. I don't think I can bear it. Not another night like last night. Not another morning like this morning. Hello? A little help in here, please?

3

Big Daddy

And nothing happens. Almost always, nothing happens; nothing at all. A big fat zero. No answering voice speaks up in the echo chamber of your skull. The morning you couldn't face comes anyway. Night falls, and the darkness of your guilt or your sorrow or your bereavement comes round again. If you happened to be crouched in a shell-crater on a battlefield when you made your experiment in prayer, on the no-atheists-in-foxholes principle, the bullets continue to zip towards you on trajectories that are perfectly unaltered. You can beat with your fists on it and the door stays locked, possibly because the thing you're asking to open isn't even a door. It's one of the walls. It's just one of the smooth, flat, hard, sintered surfaces of the state of things.

Well, we've arrived at God. Or at God's absence. I've made you wait. I started a step further back than you may have been expecting, because when we got to this point I wanted us to be arriving at Him as people do in experience: not as a philosophical proposition, an abstract possibility, but as the answer to a need, something we might yearn toward for reasons of intelligible guilt or sorrow, whether or not there's anything there to satisfy the yearning. More Hebrew poetry: 'Like as the hart desireth the waterbrooks, so longeth my soul after thee, O God.* The deer the soul's being compared to, there, is being chased by someone. It's being hunted. It's hot, and sweaty, and desperate. It has been running for a long time. It wants a mouthful of cold water it can snatch up as it runs, to keep it going a little bit further. It is not looking for a world-view. It wants, it needs, it hopes, it longs.

But what does it get in response? What do you get, when you ask? Nothing. No pannikin of cold water is brought to your thirsty lips. A lot of people conclude from this, not surprisingly, that they were foolish to ask at all. They recoil, feeling stupid. Feeling, despite themselves, a little rejected too. You ask for help and you get nothing: on a conscious level you may have decided that there was nobody there *to* help, but less consciously, since you *did* ask, it feels as if help was denied. Hence the angry edge that sometimes sharpens disbelief when it's been renewed by one of these episodes of fruitless asking. In the words of Samuel Beckett, 'He doesn't exist, the bastard!' The life of faith has just as many he-doesn't-exist-the-bastard moments as the life of disbelief. Probably more of them, if anything, given that we believers tend to return to the subject more often, producing many more opportunities to be disappointed. This is because, for us too, nothing happens when we ask for help. The nothing that happens is universal, an experience shared by believers and unbelievers alike. It

* Psalm 42.

is true that we understand the nothing differently, but not because we start from a different experience of it.

Instead it's that from the same experience a different perception grows, slowly and intermittently and (from time to time) overwhelmingly. I'm going to have to generalise freely now from my own experience, because I'm dealing with strictly internal events, and I don't have direct access to anyone else's interior. I haven't been anyone else; only myself. But I'd guess that for most of us who do end up believing, the moment when we asked and nothing happened changes in retrospect. It becomes, afterwards, part of the history of how help did after all arrive, though not in the way we were expecting it to. We look back on it and we find it altered. Its significance is different now. Literally its significance: its sign-age, the way that it points. It isn't that the story has been rewritten, with a piece of imaginary cause and effect projected back into it from some happier future point, with unreliable memory erasing the disappointments of the past by inserting a phantom helper's phantom action. That's not the feeling. It remains perfectly clear that at the moment of asking nothing happened, nothing altered in the world, nothing started up. But we begin to recognise that the moment signifies anyway, because it was then, when we asked and because we asked, that we started, falteringly, tentatively, to be able to notice something that was happening already. Something that did not need to start, it having never stopped, never paused, never faltered. Something that did (we come to see) constitute an answer; something that had been going on all the time unremarked, so steady and continuous that we had never picked it out of the general background roar of the world. I mean the roar in our minds as well as the literal clash and grind and hum of things. We live in a noisy place, inside and out, and the noise we hear pours into the noise we make. It's hard to listen, even when misery nudges you into trying.

Fortunately, the international league of the guilty has littered the landscape with specialised buildings where attention comes easier. I walk in. I glance around. And I see the objects that different ages carried in here because they thought they were precious, tattered battle flags and stained glass, carved wood and memorials saying HE WAS A MAGISTRATE OF UN-EQUALLED PROBITY: not in order to declare, those past people, that this was a place where only a precious and tasteful selection from human behaviour was welcome, but the opposite, to celebrate with the best things they had the way the place acknowledged absolutely all of human behaviour. The calm in here is not denial. It's an ancient, imperturbable lack of surprise. To any conceivable act you might have committed, the building is set up only to say, ah, so you have, so you did; yes. Would you like to sit down? I sit down. I shut my eyes.

Churches are vessels of hush, as well as everything else they are, and when I block out the distractions of vision, the silence is almost shockingly loud. It sings in my ears. Well, no; metaphors are inevitable here but we might as well try to use them accurately, and to prune out the implications we don't want. The silence has no tune. It doesn't sing. It hisses; it whines thinly at a high constant pitch, as if the world had a background note we don't usually hear. It crackles like the empty grooves at the end of a vinyl record, when the song is over and all that's left to hear is the null track of the medium itself. Which is welcome, because it's the unending song of my self that I've come in here to get a break from. I breathe in, I breathe out. I breathe in, I breathe out. I breathe in, I breathe out; noticing the action of my lungs swelling and compressing, swelling and compressing, much more than I usually do, and so far as I have to have something to concentrate on I concentrate on that, just that, the in and out of my breath, trying to think of nothing else but the air moving. I do my best to step away from my thoughts when they come, and they do come, I'm not trying to clamp them down. Every so often I find I've strayed off from the breathing along some loop of associations or memories, and that's fine. When I find that that's what I'm doing, I step away from the thought-loop, I leave it be, back to the simple process of breath. I know my whole lumpy, complicated, half-known self is still there, but I'm not trying to put it in order; I'm not trying to arrange it flatteringly, so that it tells some creditable story of me, or – just as bad, just as effortful – unflatteringly, so that it neatly accuses me. I'm deliberately abandoning the enterprise of making sense of myself. I breathe in, I breathe out. The silence hisses, neither expectantly nor unexpectantly.

And in it I start to pick out more and more noises that were too quiet for me to have attended to them before. I become intensely aware of small things happening in the space around me that I can't see. I hear a bluebottle blundering by somewhere above. I hear the door sigh open, sigh closed. I hear the creak of wood as someone else settles into a pew. I hear the intermittent murmur of a conversation going on in the vestry. I hear the sailcloth flap of a single piece of paper being turned over up in the organ loft. I start to hear things outside the church too. A passing plane. A bird in a tree. A car's ignition coughing awake. The patter-tap, patter-tap of a leafy branch the breeze is brushing against one of the windows. Two street drinkers arguing. Far-off motorway roar I must hear all the time and cancel from consciousness usually. Layer upon layer of near sounds and far sounds, stopping and starting according to no score, none of them predictable by me, none of them under my control. The audio assemblage of the world getting along perfectly well without me. The world sounding the same as it did before I was born, the same as it will do after I'm dead.

I expand. Not seeing, I feel the close grain of the hardwood I'm sitting on, the gritty solidity of the stone pillar my arm touches. I feel their real weight, I sense the labour that made them, I know their separateness from me. My mind moves outwards, to the real substances of things that are not-me beyond the church walls. I feel the churchyard grass, repeating millionfold

59

the soft green spire of each blade, the tarmac of the road compressed like cold varnished chewing gum, the scratchy roughness of each red suburban brick. Out and out, the streets of the town unreeling faster and faster into the particular pattern of fields beyond; the viridian tie-dye of those fields seen from above, and receding, higher and higher; the island, seen whole in mottled greens and browns; the limb of the planet, shining in electric blue; the ash-coloured moon; the boiling chemical clouds of the gas giants; the shining pinprick of our star; the radiant drift of the Western Spiral Arm; the plughole spin of one galaxy; the flying splotches of others, uncountably many, flinging out into a darkness which is itself expanding; and all, all of it, as locally real and solid and intricate as the time-darkened, bottom-polished oak plank beneath me. Breathe in, breathe out. Yes, time. Expand again, not from this particular place but this particular moment, this perch on one real instant in the flood of real instants. Breathe in, breathe out. Day opens the daisies, sucks carbon into every leaf, toasts the land, raises moisture as clouds. Night closes flowers, throws the protein switch for rest in mobile creatures, condenses dew, pulls the winds that day has pushed. Breathe. Dark cycles into light, light cycles into dark again as the earth turns, and this cycle measured in hours spins inside others timed in weeks and years and aeons, building a nested spirograph of change of which the world is made as truly as it's made of matter organised in a sphere. The fields flash green-yellow-brown with the seasons. The forests ebb and flow. The hills themselves melt like wax. The ice advances and retreats, ocean covers this spot with sunlit shallows or anoxic black depths. The carbon fixed by a trillion tiny swimmers hardens as limestone and erodes gently to gas again. Natural selection whittles new creatures from old with its blunt knife. And it's all real. The moments that happen already to have happened were as capacious, as strutted and braced with true existence, as this one in which I am momentarily sitting here, and the moments which happen not to have happened yet will be in their turn as truly and encompassingly the one single existent entire state of things, just for a moment. This instant at which I sit is as narrow a slice of the reality of the whole as a hairline crack would be in a pavement that reaches to the stars. The real immensities of time and of space merge; are – always were – the same real immensity.

But now it gets indescribable. Now I register something that precedes all this manifold immensity that is not-me and yet is real; something makes itself felt from beyond or behind or beneath it all. What can 'beyond' or 'behind' or 'beneath' mean, when all possible directions or dimensions are already included in the sum of what is so? I don't know. I've only got metaphors to work with, and this is where metaphor, which compares one existing thing to another thing, is being asked to reach beyond its competence. Beyond, again: but I'm not talking about movement through or out of any of the shapes of existing things. I'm talking about a movement through or out of shape altogether, yet not into vacuum, not into emptiness. Into fullness rather. Into an adjacent fullness, no further away than the thickness of everything, which feels now as if, in this direction that can't be stated, it is no thickness at all. It feels as if, considered this way, every solid thing is as thin as a film in its particular being, and is backed onto some medium in which the journey my attention's been taking, toward greater and greater solidity, richer and richer presence, reaches an absolute. What's in front is real; what's behind is the reason for it being real, the source of its realness. Beyond, behind, beneath all solid things there seems to be solidity. Behind, beneath, beyond all changes, all wheeling and whirring processes, all flows, there seems to be flow itself. And though I'm in the dark behind my closed eyelids, and light is part of the everything it feels as if I'm feeling beyond, so can only be a metaphor here, it seems to shine, this universal backing to things, with light-less light, or dark light; choose your paradox. It feels as if everything is backed with light, everything floats on a sea of light, everything is just a surface feature of the light. And that includes me. Every tricky thing I am, my sprawling piles of memories and secrets and misunderstandings, float on the sea; are local corrugations and whorls with the limitless light just behind. And now I've forgotten to breathe, because the shining something, an infinitesimal distance away out of the universe, is breathing in me and through me, and though the experience is grand beyond my powers to convey, it's not impersonal. Someone, not something, is here. Though it's on a scale that defeats imagining and exists without location (or exists in all locations at once) I feel what I feel when there's someone beside me. I am being looked at. I am being known; known in some wholly accurate and complete way that is only possible when the point of view is not another local self in the world but glows in the whole medium in which I live and move. I am being seen from inside, but without any of my own illusions. I am being seen from behind, beneath, beyond. I am being read by what I am made of.

On one level I can feel that this is absolutely safe. A parent's safe hold is nothing compared to this. I'm being carried on the universe's shoulder. But on another level, it's terrifying. Being screened off by my separateness is all I know in my dealings with somebodies who look at me. This is utterly exposed. And while it may be safe, it is not kind in one of the primary ways in which human beings set about being kind to each other. It takes no account, at all, of my illusions about myself. It lays me out, roofless, wall-less, worse than naked. It knows where my kindness comes chequered with secret cruelties or mockeries. It knows where my love comes with reservations. It knows where I hate, and fear, and despise. It knows what I indulge in. It knows what parasitic colonies of habit I have allowed to form in me. It knows the best of me, which may well be not what I am proud of, and the worst of me, which is not what it has occurred to me to be ashamed of. It

knows what I have forgotten. It knows all this, and it
shines at me. In fact it never stops shining. It is continuous, this attention it pays. I cannot make it turn
away. But I can turn away from it, easily; all I have to
do is to stop listening to the gentle, unendingly patient
call it stitches through the fabric of everything there is.
It compels nothing, so all I have to do is stop paying attention. And I do, after not very long. I can't bear, for
very long at once, to be seen like that. To be seen like
that is judgement in itself. As a long-ago letter writer
put it, someone who clearly went where I've just been,
it is terrible to fall into the hands of the living God.
Only, to be seen like that is forgiveness too – or at any
rate, the essential beginning of forgiveness; and when
I come back from the place where the metaphors end,
and the light behind light shines, and I open my eyes
in the quiet church, for a little while everything I see
glows as if it were lamplit from inside, and every flowing particle of the whole gleams in its separate grains;
gleams as if it were treasured.

Do I feel better? It depends what you mean by 'better'. As my godfather asked suspiciously when a nurse
said it to him, 'Better than what?' I don't feel cuddled,
soothed, flattered; I don't feel distracted or enter-
tained. My fancy has not been tickled. I have not been
shown cool huge stuff by a very big version of Jerry
Bruckheimer. I have not been meddled with, or repro-
grammed, or had my settings tweaked. I have not been
administered a cosmic antidepressant. I have not had
my HPtFtU removed by magic. I have not been told to

take it easy because I'm OK and you're OK. Instead I have been shown the authentic bad news about myself, in a perspective which is so different from the tight focus of my desperation that it is good news in itself; I have been shown that though I may see myself in the grim optics of sorrow and self-dislike, I am being seen all the while, if I can bring myself to believe it, with a generosity wider than oceans. I've been gently and implacably reminded of how little I know a whole truth about myself. I've been made unfamiliar to my-self, and therefore hopeful; I've had the grip of des-peration loosened. Desperation may well come back. In fact it may only feel as if desperation has slackened by one infinitesimal notch, but it has slackened, it has eased, because just for now I have been enabled to feel beyond it, or rather to participate a little bit in the free-dom of a feeling that flows beyond, behind, beneath, around it.* This is comfort, but it is not comfortable. It is awkward, undignified, exposed, risky-feeling. It is like finding that there is something in the thin air to lean on, something in the void – something *about* the void – which will hold you up, but only if you tip your-self madly forward onto it and ask it to take your weight.

Now, I can assemble as easily as anyone an account of what just happened to me in the church which is purely, unmysteriously physical. Yes, the mild sensory

---

* Yes, I'm talking about essentially the same experience that I had with the Mozart in Chapter One. In some ways, God is a bit of a one-trick pony.

deprivation I subjected myself to by sitting for half an hour or so with my eyes shut will have prompted the bits of my brain that handle visual imagery to start working up pictures from whatever inputs they could get, from memory and association and imagination. Yes, the deliberate breathing probably made me hyper-ventilate slightly, and flushed me through with exciting oxygen. Yes, the emotional state I was in will have made me suggestible. Yes, the feeling that another person is present is a common feature of mental states more relaxed than ordinary consciousness: it happens quite a lot on the verge of sleep, for example. Yes, I know that we all have an evolved tendency to detect personhood or agency in environments, whether or not it is actually there. Since we find faces in wallpaper and puddles of spilled cappuccino, my discovery of consciousness beneath the skin of the universe will not have been much of a stretch, cognitively speaking. Yes, I imagine that my pupils dilated while my eyes were shut, and then when I opened them again the photons flooded in through an unusually wide aperture. Yes, I'm sure that I would have felt very similar things if you had crept up on me while I sat and applied a powerful magnetic field to the appropriate area of my head. Or if I'd just swallowed an E. Result: one 're-ligious experience' delivered to order, complete with lightshow. In fact, in terms of sensation I'm sure the magnetic field and pill would have been far more re-liable, because I wouldn't have been dependent on my own paltry, stop-and-go brain chemistry.

But so what? These are explanations of how my feelings might have arisen, physically, but they don't explain my feelings away. They don't prove that my feelings were not really my feelings. They certainly don't prove that there was nobody there for me to be feeling them about. If God does exist, then from my point of view it's hard to see how a physical creature like myself could ever register His presence *except* through some series or other of physically-determined bodily states. I'm not an abstract being. Everything I feel, I feel by way of hormones and neurotransmitters and nerve fibres. Starting to believe in God is a lot like falling in love, and there is certainly a biochemical basis for *that*. Cocktails of happy hormones make you gooey and trusting; floods of neurotransmitters make your thoughts skip elatedly along. Does this prove that the person you love is imaginary? It does not. The most the physical accounts demonstrate, where God is concerned, is that He isn't *necessary* as an explanation. Which I feel does not really amount to news. I kind of knew that anyway, my philosophical starting-point for all this being that we don't *need* God to explain any material aspect of the universe, including our mental states; while conversely, no material fact about the universe is ever going to decide for us whether He exists. God's non-necessity in explanations is a given, for me. For me, it means that I'm only ever going to get to faith by some process quite separate from proof and disproof; that I'm only going to arrive at it because, in some way that it is not in the power of evidence to rebut, it feels right.

For you, on the other hand, it may seem amazingly obvious, blatantly and overwhelmingly obvious, that I *cannot* really have been feeling the presence of God. Because, even if final degrees of proof or disproof remain out of reach, such a thing would be vanishingly, microscopically unlikely compared to the probability that one, several, or all of the physical factors above were deluding me into giving houseroom to hocus-pocus. If this is so, I would respectfully ask you to examine your conviction, and in particular to have a look at the relative roles played in it by argument and by an emotional position of your own. There *are* arguments to be made about God based on probability* but

---

* Though the good ones do not include the steaming heap of 'evolutionary' manure raked together by Richard Dawkins, or Bertrand Russell's teapot. Oh dear, must I really engage with these, given that I'm not trying to play the game of proof and disproof? I suppose I must. I may not be interested in proof – you can't disprove the existence of a feeling – but I am interested in the feeling's philosophical dignity. I do want to assert that it doesn't have the status of reality-denial, that it doesn't exist in blatant defiance of some obvious demonstration of its groundlessness. So, then, at speed: Richard Dawkins claims that God's existence is improbable because the creator of the universe would have to be really complicated. The only way we know of to get complicated creatures is via natural selection, and natural selection can't have operated before the universe began. QED? Nah. When people who believe in God talk about God, we don't mean that a being exists who is an animal like ourselves, only bigger and cleverer and more complex. We don't think He lives in the universe. In fact we don't think that He exists in any environment; we don't imagine that He had to grow, or evolve, or appear, or emerge, thanks to some process or other. It's the other way up. We think that all processes exist thanks to Him;

for a lot of people they function as a rationalisation after the event for a deep and emotional conviction that the universe is just not the kind of place in which such things can happen. An experience of the presence of God is just not compatible with an instinctual sense of what the world is like. For a lot of people, the world is constituted by stable, dependable, familiar sense-experiences among which it is self-evident that there's no room for radical strangeness, for breaches of context. 'I don't believe in any gods,' some New Atheists

---

we think that He is the universe's environment. We may well be wrong, crazed, doolally, travelling first-class on the delusion express, but showing that God-the-evolved-organism is unlikely says nothing about the probability of the different thing we do in fact believe. Arguing with people imposes an unfortunate necessity to find out what they think before you open your big mouth to contradict it. Next, the teapot. Russell said that those who staked the intellectual integrity of belief on the impossibility of disproving God's existence were like people suggesting that there was an undetectable teapot in orbit between the earth and Mars. No one sensible would regard the claim as anything but vanishingly unlikely. Just because you couldn't definitely show the pot was absent, its spout not slowly tracing out circles as the solar wind blew on it, its glaze not gleaming faintly in the reflected starlight, it didn't mean you had to take it seriously. You could be sure enough the teapot wasn't there to leave it at that; likewise God. QED? Again, nope, because the Russellian teapot argument commits the fallacy of assuming the state of the universe it seeks to demonstrate. Russell would *like* claims about God to be as obviously trivial and inconsequential as the teapot. But the appropriateness of the comparison rests on a prior judgement: and if it really matters as little as all that whether there's a God or not, you have to wonder why it's worth writing whole books trying to dispel him. It's not as if anyone has bothered to publish *The Teapot Delusion*. May I recommend instead, for anyone who wants to explore better probability-based arguments against God, the website www.lesswrong.com? In particular, the post titled 'Absence of evidence *is* evidence of absence'.

like to say, ingeniously lower-casing a quite large proposition about the universe into a zoological category which it's easy to show is empty.

I don't believe in any gods, I think they're saying, because I *do* believe in the felt completeness, the experienced adequacy, of a world of supermarket trolleys, hangovers, suburban Sundays, toothache, drum 'n' bass, romantic love, diminishing marginal utility and the smell of fresh paint. This world is solid, stolid even. It makes no sudden moves. It incorporates an absolutely firm distinction between a prosaic, law-governed external reality and a private, internal domain of imagination which exerts no traction over prosaic reality except by prosaic means – by the publication of fantasy novels, for instance. This world believes that it has science on its side. Indeed, by an act of oblivious metaphorical digestion, it tends to believe that it *is* science; it thinks that what it sees around it is the bare, disenchanted, unmediated, uncoloured truth delivered by the scientific method. Look, no gods! Also, no fairies, no unicorns, no griffins, no leprechauns. A quick census of the local fauna confirms it: case solved. But this perceptual world *isn't* science. It is a cultural artefact created by one version of the cultural influence of science, specific to the last two centuries in Europe and North America. It is not a direct, unmediated picture of reality; far from it. It is a drastically human-centred, human-scaled selection from the physical universe, comfortably restricted to the order of reality which is cooked rather than raw, which happens within the envelope of society. It scarcely touches on what the world is like apart from us. It doesn't acknowledge the radical strangeness of quantum mechanics, down in reality's basement; it doesn't engage with the perturbing immensity of cosmology, up in the attic; it doesn't admit the extraordinary temporariness of even the familiar things we think we possess securely on our middle floor of the universe. It treats us living creatures as the securely-tenured lords of all we survey, rather than as the brief ripples of information we actually amount to. In fact the stolid 'science' of this obviously godless world is rather eighteenth-century. Needless to say, none of the proven strangenesses of the physical universe make the existence of God any likelier (or less likely). They imply nothing about it at all. I am not one of those soft-brained purveyors of New Age woo who propose that if some weird things are true, any weird thing you think of can be true. All I'm pointing out is that if the basis for your conviction that there's no room for God is the comfy familiarity of the universe, it's a bit of a problem if it turns out not to be comfortable or familiar.

What I do find troubling, though, is the uncertainty of the experience I'm talking about: the way it is, tremblingly, only just there, the way it slips out of definite reach, the way it eludes definition. Even the description of it I've given here has firmed it up considerably. I've put it into words when it didn't happen in words, and thereby taken a decision-making editorial grip on something which, at the time, I couldn't grip or make decisions about at all. Reading over what I've written, I fear I've turned it into an *effect*, a special effect in prose, controlled by me. It wasn't one, and it wasn't controlled by me. It was a shimmer of sensation. One of those seems a flimsy foundation to rest anything on, let alone a huge and ponderous thing like an organised religion: two thousand years of Christian ideas and stories and practices making a vast stone pyramid, all balanced upside down on its point, on a fulcrum of mere feeling. It doesn't seem much on which to build an institution. It doesn't seem much to rest a way of living on. But that's the way it is. The whole thing is – has to be – uncertain right down to the root. The whole thing has to remain as flimsy as you judge the experience of God's presence to be. When I'm only trying to remember the feeling of it – right now, for example – I myself am often as sure as makes no difference that it's all moonshine and muscle cramps. That there's nothing there at all. That he doesn't exist, the bastard. Yet what it has felt like when I *have* felt it cannot be pushed aside. It goes on working in me, this experience, whatever my changing opinion about it happens to be; it has altered my conviction of what the universe is like, way down deep, too deep for he-doesn't-exist-the-bastard to erase it. It has had consequences in me. That's what I need to convey and probably can't: that this is something so elusive that you can't securely put your finger on it, and yet at the same time is so strongly felt, when it is felt, that it illuminates the world and reorganises a life. It's elusive and it's a foundation. It's a wisp of presence, as deniable as vapour, which you feel is holding the house up. It's a presence which may well not be there, but which can draw out of you, when you feel it, a trust that it is the thing which precedes all things, us included; that it is first, and last, and largest, and lowest; that it exists without terms and conditions. That you can come to it in need and know that you're forgiven.* That it shines.

And what comes next, if you've felt this? Well, as I've said, it won't bother you if you don't bother it. It is as easy to ignore as the air. But if you find your way to it again, it will be there again. You can't stay there for long, but it stays there for ever. It is tireless, it is permanent. And (mostly) the more often you find your way to it, the easier the way becomes, until your private signposts to the path there become part of the texture of things you expect, on the inside of your head. You get used to the faint whisper of presence, in the direction that is no-direction. You start to try to feel out the dimensions of the experience, to work out what follows from this alarming thing: what you can know about it, what (if anything) you should do about it. What it implies. This, for the first time, is where the organised material of religion can come into the picture, because

---

* I've left out an extremely important aspect of how this works, which I'll come to in Chapter Five. Good grief, I'm editing God for the sake of explanatory effectiveness.

what you've experienced is an absolutely bog-standard piece of transcendence, common to all cultures, from which many different structures of meaning have been unfolded in different times and different places. The light-without-light, the sense of being understood – it's what Hindus feel, and Buddhists, and Zoroastrians, and Jains, and Shinto believers, as well as those of us in the three sibling religions that name the presence as God. Which is what you'd expect, if the whole thing were being generated by a common feature of *Homo sapiens* brain chemistry; but which is also what you'd expect if the species were making a common response to an aspect of reality. The process by which the universal experience takes on the contours of a particular religion is partly passive, just a matter of colour leaking in from the surrounding culture, just a matter of adopting the interpretation that dominates in your local environment. But it's also a process of co-operation, a conversation between the experience and a tradition in which the test is always recognition. Do you recognise in the experience what the tradition is talking about? Is there an overlap which encourages you to give some cautious, provisional credence to the stuff the tradition is telling you which you yourself have not experienced yet? If you're a free adult, you do not assent to doctrine because authority tells you to. In terms of commanding blind obedience, I'm glad to say, we are now in the valuable position of being able to tell authority to sod off. No: you begin to think you might be willing to go along with an idea because it seems to you to translate into a statement something that has passed the test of feeling. You begin to think there is something worth possessing in a scripture because (as well as all the other things it may be) it is also palpably a report (or set of reports) from a place you have been to on your own account. I myself am a Christian and not a Muslim or a Buddhist for a mixture of the two different kinds of reason; as an outcome of both kinds of process. On the passive side, Christianity was the religion of my childhood. It's the ancient religion, for something like forty generations, of the place I come from. It's the matrix of my culture. But it's also something I came back to, freely, as an adult, after twenty-odd years of atheism, because piece by piece I have found that it answers my need, and corresponds to emotional reality for me. I also find that the elaborated structure of meaning it builds, the story it tells, explains that reality more justly, more profoundly, more scrupulously and plausibly than any of the alternatives. (Am I sure I'm right? Of course not. Don't you get bored with asking that question?)

A lot of what you learn comes direct from the feeling. You reflect on it, and you find out about it. You find out what kinds of description of it can perhaps be true. You find out what descriptions of it can't possibly be true. For instance: is it like having an imaginary friend? Well, yes and no. Yes, in that it can't be denied that the whisper of presence in your head, when you attend to it, makes you feel that you're in company even when you're physically alone. But no, in that the presence which gleams intermittently in your mind doesn't chatter cosily on, making conversation, endorsing your judgements, helping you to whistle bravely in the dark, being what you want an ideally understanding friend to be. It doesn't say: they're all meanies, but *I* love you. It doesn't say: yes Tony, yes George, I want you to invade Iraq *right now*. In fact it doesn't speak at all, in my experience. And it doesn't feel, at all, as if it is available for ventriloquism. You can't stick your metaphorical hand up its metaphorical back and waggle its metaphorical jaws, while projecting onto it some message you'd like to hear. Of all the personalities to whom we might lend headspace when they aren't physically present – the little inboard simulacra of the people we love, the remembered dead, Mr Knightley, Obi-wan Kenobi – this is the one in whose mouth it seems least plausible to put words of our own. It is not ours to play with. It is other.

Which may seem a little strange as a statement, when I so clearly suggested at the beginning of this chapter that people look for God because they're hoping, they're yearning, they're wishing for His existence. Doesn't that imply that the God we wish for will behave, when we think we've found Him, like a wish fulfilled? Gratifying us, being what we wish Him to be, modelling Himself to our expectations with squishy responsiveness? That's certainly the infantile image of God that New Atheists promulgate, God as an image of our own need imprinted onto the soft jelly of the universe. But – nope. We wish for God to exist, but we don't wish for Him to exist *as* a wish, scattering fairy dust to order. And in this logic is on our side. Follow me closely now: whether God exists or not is unprovable, so for an individual person, whether He exists or not is always going to be a matter of belief. But at the same time, quite independently, He either exists or He doesn't, irrespective of whether He's believed in. He's a fact, or a non-fact, about the nature of the universe. So if you believe, you're making a bet that God exists whether you believe or not. If you believe, you're not perceiving God as a creature of your belief, called into being by it, ebbing and flowing as it ebbs and flows. You're perceiving a state of the universe. You may be wrong, but if you are wrong, you're not wrong because of your emotional motives for belief, you're not wrong because you're weak and credulous. You're just wrong. Likewise, if you're right, you're not right because of anything you did or felt, because there was anything deserving or admirable about your feelings. You just are right. I realise this may come as a shock, but wishing does not in fact cause things to exist. Or to cease to exist. If something does exist, then wishing for that something does not infect it with wishfulness.

But the logic here is just giving an abstract demonstration of what, in my experience, you possess as a very un-abstract emotion. One of the things you can feel you are sure of about this presence is that it doesn't behave like any kind of straightforward projection of your own attributes. It won't be fixed, bounded, tied down that way. It won't stay within the limits of any particular piece of your imagining. Any description you may give of it, it exceeds. It is always different from what you expected: not because your expectations are necessarily wrong, but because it is always *more than* them. It offers an ocean when you propose a glass of water. It feels as if having even the ghost of a hint of a taste of a suggestion of it in your mind requires a spatially impossible contortion in which the immense is contained in the tiny. If you try to imagine what the world is like from its point of view you stumble into awe, defeated.

This is a feeling that seems to tell against the impression people often have that 'God' is a device for infusing comfortable human qualities into the vast, cold cosmos. The science-fiction writer Adam Roberts put the point very wittily in a recent novel: 'I enjoy eating beefsteaks, and because beefsteaks serve the useful purpose of keeping me alive, I therefore declare the universe to be beefsteak, God a beefsteak, and beefsteak the universal core value of everything.' He's taking the piss, of course, out of the high valuation humans tend to set on love. Christianity is dead set[*] on God being loving, and being Love, which may indeed be a bizarre category error: one little species busily projecting its concerns out onto vast material indifference, moseying on up to neutron stars and saying hey, let's talk about heartbreak. But again, that's not what it feels like. It doesn't feel, at least in my experience, as if 'declaring' is what's going on.

---

[*] Pun intended.

Or asserting, or deciding, or selecting, or any of the active, uh, activities that would be involved in using religion as a hand mirror we hold up to view our own faces. Here the big difference between monotheism and polytheism comes in, because in polytheism you do have a form of religion which projects human attributes; where, in fact, projecting human attributes is pretty much the point.

Greek and Roman and Norse paganism provided – sometimes the modern Wiccan variety too provides – a way to acknowledge the power of the impulses that buffet us within and without, by turning them into capitalised Powers. Many-god religions separate out and purify human qualities, and then concentrate them into mythological figures who express each quality in blazing, drastic, unmediated form. For love, a goddess of love. For rage, a god of war. For motherhood, fatherhood, wisdom, justice, death, vengeance, craft, boundary-making, youth, music, healing, language – a god or goddess each. And you can see that this can make for a very effective tool of self-understanding, not on the analytical level but concretely and immediately, down deep where stories live. The pantheons of polytheism give you something like a card pack or Tarot pack of potent figures, which the myths deal out again and again, each deal, each arrangement, each story having the potential to reveal some legible new aspect of the relationship between the powers that jostle and feud within us. Polytheism honours the range of what we are. Which is nice.

But quite egocentric. And it's not what the shimmer of presence in my mind feels like, with its universal backing for everything, its imperturbably equal support for a fabric of being stretching far beyond and away from our preoccupations. Which is one reason why it makes sense to me to interpret the shimmer not as the presence of *a* god, some local force from our psyche's back catalogue, but as *the* God, Ha Shem, Ho Theos, Al-Lah, dimly and locally perceived as He (She, It) goes about His (Her, Its) unimaginable business of being the ground and origin of everything.

Everything meaning really everything, not some broad-sounding but secretly uplifting selection from everything. Monotheism can't pick and choose the nice bits – or the interesting bits, or the impressive bits, or any particular category of bits of existence at all. It can't, as one unexpected consequence, be tasteful. Or let's put it more strongly, since saying 'tasteful' may sound as if I'm claiming some kind of avant-garde, *épatez-les-bourgeois* virtue here, which only disrupts twee or kitsch or chocolate-boxy versions of good taste. Let's say, it can't be beautiful, or it can't ever only be beautiful, according to whatever serious standard of beauty you care to specify. It can't do this –

Under the sliding star signs she fills the ship-laden sea and the fruitful earth with her being; through her the generations are conceived and rise up to see the sun; from her the storm clouds flee; to her the earth, the skilful maker, offers

flowers. The wide levels of the sea smile at her,
and all the quiet sky shines and streams with
light . . .

– which is the Roman poet Lucretius praising the goddess Venus, as recently translated by the American
writer Ursula Le Guin. The God of everything can't
claim this kind of beautifully matched suite of natural
moods and natural moments and natural symbols. A
goddess of fertility can have picked out for her the
peaceful, the smiling parts of natural fruitfulness; she
can have attributed to her what the growing and
breeding of the living world feels like on a calm bright
day in spring. But the God of everything must be
manifest *in* everything.

Just to stay in the domain of living processes and
the reproduction thereof: as well as backing the existence of roses and kittens, the God of everything must
sustain tapeworms, necrotising bacteria that reduce
flesh to a puddle of pus, and parasitic wasps as they
eat their way out of their hosts. Any cell that divides
in any organism must be doing so in the radiance
of the universal attention. Our judgements of beauty
and utility and desirability are beside the point. Cro-
cuses multiply, and so do anthrax spores, and the
God of everything smiles on all alike. The same has
to be true of all the acts and events of human societies; and of all places, and of all times; and in fact
of every configuration of matter and energy everywhere, continuously. The God of everything must be

equally present for everything. You name it. He is exactly as present in a room in a failing strip-mall where a malfunctioning fluorescent tube is jittering out headache for all onlookers as He is in a cathedral. He pays equal attention to the individual way each of the billion separate pebbles lie on a pebble beach. And on all the other beaches. He knows and sustains the exact placement of every single molecule of frozen carbon dioxide in the northern polar cap of Mars. And of every other molecule of every other planet, around every other star. The lot. For every unselected speck of existence, patient shining.

Now I seem to be coming perilously close to the sycophantic prayer in *Monty Python's Meaning of Life*. You know the one I mean: 'Oh God, you are so very, very big. So absolutely huge. Oh Lord, you really are gigantic . . . ' But, unencompassable though the God of everything must be to a human imagination, it doesn't seem to be the case in my experience that you respond to Him (Her, It) as if He were some looming giant requiring to be admired and praised and buttered up; anxiously complimented on His bulk. There's some fear there, all right, but it's not the fear you feel for power when you encounter a powerful force or a powerful person in the world. It's more like the fear you might feel for an overwhelming landscape, where the palpable bigness around you makes it clear you are amidst something that does not operate within your limits. The God of everything's omnipresence in time can do this just as much as His omnipresence in space; maybe more so, given the short shelf-life of awe compared to our permanent preoccupation with the chronological limits on our existence. If there is an attention that was shining away fully-formed at the t-zero moment when the universe began, then it must also, more to the point, have been steadily holding everything in being at the moment when you yourself were conceived; and it will still be shining on, unchanged, unaged, unexhausted, at the moment when your last breath sighs out on the hospice bed. And for all the ages afterwards. Something that does not begin and does not end can be a fearful prospect, for creatures like us who do both. Yet more Hebrew poetry:

> As for man, his days are as grass. As a flower of the field, so he flourisheth. For the wind passeth over it, and it is gone; and the place thereof shall know it no more. But the mercy of the Lord is from everlasting unto everlasting upon them that fear him . . .

Humility is one option here – the urge to kneel, or to sit very quietly, conscious of your microscopic brevity in relation to what is visiting you. Another option is resentment, at this impervious immortal *thing* that is immune to our mortality. (And doesn't even exist, the bastard.) But humiliation – the sensation of being forcibly reduced or pressed down by power – doesn't seem to come into it. It doesn't seem to be in the nature of the presence you're feeling that it should make you feel crushed or abject. It has no designs on your dignity, perhaps because of the way in which the power of the God of everything differs from all the other manifestations of power you'll ever meet. This power is not exercised from the top of any hierarchy. It does not radiate from any local point within the universe at all. It works entirely through presence. Kings and caliphs, emperors and popes, televangelists and household bullies have all wanted to claim that their authority is a licensed copy of its universal reach, but their claim must always be incomplete at best. In the end, their power and His are unlike. Their power is rivalrous, in the economic sense. It is big because others' power is small. It needs to be extracted from the submission of other apes like themselves. But His power needs nothing, competes with nothing, compels nothing, exists at nothing's expense. You could no more be humiliated by Him (Her, It) than you could by the height of the Himalayas or the depth of the Atlantic or the number of oxygen atoms in the air. It may make sense to compare Him to a king, if a king is your best local image of unparalleled majesty, but even if He is like a king, kings are not like Him.* He is more than any

---

* A discovery which has had profound historical consequences. There's a direct line from 'Long live Christ the King!' to 'No king but King Jesus!' to the rediscovery of republicanism in modern Europe and North America.

king. He is as common as the air. He is the ordinary ground. And yet a presence. And yet a person.

When is it that you can say you believe? It's tricky, since belief is often so intermittent; is so often chequered through or stippled through with disbelief; is so much something come upon, or sensed out of the corner of the mind's eye, rather than securely possessed. Is it when you feel you've found something? Or is it much earlier: when you feel the need that will make you start looking? When you do start looking? When you fail to find anything and yet somehow don't give up the hope that you might find something some day? Maybe it's when you hope at all, in this direction.

But one point at which you can *know* you've started to believe is the point at which the tentative houseroom or headroom you're giving to the God of everything starts to have emotional consequences of its own. Problematic consequences; uncomfortable consequences; unpleasant consequences. Because if the bastard *does* exist, if the God of everything *is* shining patiently in every room, then you can't escape the truth that He must be shining in some horrible places. He must be lending his uncritical sustaining power to rooms in which the vilest things are happening. There He must be, obligingly maintaining the flow of electrons through the rusty wires that are conducting 240 volts into the soft tissue of some poor screaming soul in a torture chamber. There He must be, benignly silent, as a migrant worker is raped at a truck stop. There

He must be, shining contentedly away, in the overrun emergency room where the children from a crushed school bus are dying.

And when you've noticed that you're ready for the next act in the emotional drama of belief we're following here.* Which is, of course, horrified disgust.

---

* One of the several possible such dramas, of course. I can just follow this one with particular confidence because it happens to be mine.

4

Hello, Cruel World

As you may remember if you ever read the book version of *The Silence of the Lambs*, Hannibal Lecter collects church collapses. 'Did you see the recent one in Sicily? Marvellous! The facade fell on sixty-five grandmothers at a special Mass.' Dr Lecter likes the thud and squelch of falling masonry because it seems to suggest that, if anyone is in charge of the universe, it must be a being as cruelly, capriciously amused by human suffering as he is himself. You look up in the naive hope of love and protection, and back comes your answer: a bus-sized chunk of baroque stonework. What's more, as Lecter delightedly notes, it's actually faith that creates the black joke here. Without faith, there'd be nothing but indifferent material forces at work. It's only when the idea of events having an author is introduced that the universe becomes cruel, as opposed to merely heavy, or fast-moving, or prone to unpredictable acceleration. 'Was that evil? If so, who did it? If He's up there, He just loves it, Officer Starling. Typhoid and swans, it all comes from the same place.'

It's faith that creates the 'problem of pain', as the whole issue is known in theological shorthand: the whole problem of suffering's existence in a world supposedly presided over by a loving and all-powerful God. In the absence of God, of course, there's still pain. But there's no problem. It's just what happens. Once the God of everything is there in the picture, and the physics and biology and history of the world we know become in some ultimate sense His responsibility, the lack of love and protection in the order of things begins to shriek out. If the universe is a made thing, instead of an accidental thing, it only takes a fairly short adult acquaintance with it for it to be obvious that it is, in certain respects, very badly made. It is intricately, beautifully, wonderfully made; but also carelessly, dangerously, clumsily made. And aswarm with cruelties. There is no finessing this. No matter how remote you believe God is from the day-to-day management of the cosmos – and for me He's pretty damn remote, withdrawn from the whole thing as a condition of it existing at all – He still bears a maker's responsibility for what goes on inside it. It doesn't help to know, as almost all Christians have known for 150 years now, that God didn't design living creatures. Evolution doesn't let Him off the hook. He is still the creator and the sustainer of the processes by which life takes its myriads of altering forms, and therefore answerable for the results of those processes. And for their costs. The only easy way out of the problem is to discard the expectation that causes the problem, by ditching the author Himself. After all, there's no logical need for Him anyway. But then there's that shining, there's that glimmer, there's that never-ending song of loving intent threaded through the substrate of things; and if you find you can't discard *that*, the cruelties of the world are an emotional, not just a logical, challenge.

They can flatten you any time, given our palpable lack of protection against harm, our evident exposure to any wind of misfortune that may chance to blow on our soft and vulnerable selves. From meteor strikes to car crashes, falling masonry to early-onset Alzheimer's, anything can happen to us and to the people we love. At any moment you can have it sharply demonstrated to you that where we live, events are not governed by what people deserve. But maybe as a theme, as subject-matter for anxiety, the world's cruelties are most likely to press on you fairly early on in your history as a believer, if you're travelling on anything like my emotional path. In that case it was an awareness of the painful crappiness of things, including your own motives, that sent you seeking comfort in the first place. You were looking for help with the dismal amalgam of things you'd fucked up, in accordance with the HPtFtU, and things other people had bent or broken, and things that just seemed to arrive in a pre-spoiled state, oven-ready for disaster. And quite quickly, therefore, it probably occurs to you that there's a slight contradiction (to say the least) in seeking that comfort from the party who is Himself finally responsible for the crappiness in question. You are a character calling out for pity from the author, because you don't like the plot. But it's His plot, supposedly. So what is this, masochism? A version of Stockholm Syndrome, where you identify with your kidnapper? A defensive idealisation of an abusive parent? Daddy is kind; he has to leave me here to fight with his dogs for scraps . . .

I meant when I got to this point to describe in detail

two or three concrete instances in which the world is malignantly, unspeakably, indefensibly unpleasant. You know the kind of thing. Look at any medical encyclopedia. But I can't face it, and in any case the cruelties that strike us most deeply tend to be individual to us, and to be obvious to us too. They don't need researching, they don't need working up.

Besides, there are so many of them. There are whole multiple categories of outrage, all coded deep into the structures of existence and experience, until it can feel as if the whole thing is like a stick of seaside rock with the words HA HA HA written through it. To start with there are all the outrages of human history, all the times when the weak are abused, all the moments when intervention by an omnipotent friend of the helpless would be desperately justified, and yet is never forthcoming. It seems only fair to quote another bit of Hebrew poetry, here – 'A thousand shall fall to your left, and a thousand to your right, but the evil shall not come nigh thee . . . ' – and to point out that this psalm's picture of a God who pops a protective forcefield over those he cares about on the battlefield is *not true*, except in terms of the wishful thinking of survivorship bias, which ensures that all war stories are told by people who didn't die. It is demonstrably *not the case* that anyone goes to war with a magic grant of immunity. (And even if someone did, what about the thousands to the left and to the right, eh? What are they, chopped liver? What about the life-stories of which they are the centre, and in which they are the ones speaking the psalm? The God of everything must be the God of all stories.) The score of interventions at history's dark points is resoundingly low. Number of cattle-trucks halted on their way to the gas chamber by a fiery angel: zero. Number of smirking conquistadors, Khmer Rouge executioners, Hutu militiamen to be gently restrained by an unseen force: zero. We do our violence unimpeded. We suffer it unprotected.

Then there are the outrages of the biosphere. I don't just mean all the specific cases where parasitism or predation entails immense, unanaesthetised everyday pain – starting the roll-call, perhaps, with the caterpillar Darwin watched being eaten alive by wasp larvae, causing his famous reflection on the 'low and horridly cruel' ways of nature. I also mean the outrages inherent in the entire operation of the domain of life. The intrinsic outrages. Natural selection, as Richard Dawkins has beautifully shown us, is a sculptor of astonishing reach, capable of adapting living things to the mould of almost any environment. And all its complex effects are achieved by the millionfold iteration of a simple process; simple and horrible. Species adapt and subdivide and flourish and are extinguished, the phenotype melts like wax and reappears again transformed, because individual organisms with minute variations are 'selected' by the test of survival. But most are not selected, otherwise selection could do nothing to produce adaptive change. Most are discarded. Most organisms, by the billion, by the trillion, die or are killed before they can reproduce, dumbly eliminated by some environment's demand* for a quality they lack, whatever else they may happen to have going for them in terms of lovely feathers, iridescent wing casings, or interesting mathematical theories. The moral scandal of evolution is not that it contradicts some sweet old myth about God knitting the coats for the little lambkins: it's that it works by, works through, would not work without, continuous suffering. Suffering is not incidental to evolution. Suffering is the method. The world wobbles onward, you might say, on a trackway paved with little bones. But that understates the issue. There is no trackway – there's just the way the world happens to go, lurching one way, lurching the other. The whole landscape is little bones.

We, sapient species that we are, are inclined to take this personally, and to find a special outrage in the fact of our own mortality, especially if we're of a metaphysical disposition, or Philip Larkin. We really don't like the idea that our consciousness might just be an epiphenomenon of our DNA, generated for a few years for the sake of the tactical advantages it confers, but redundant once our children are viable alone, and thus quickly destined for oblivion. It spreads so wide, while it lasts, our consciousness; it encompasses so much. It's such a lightshow, while the soft jellies of our seeing eyes are open. So many different dawns, such a blaze and a blur

---

* All metaphor, of course: the environment is not a conscious actor. It's just a situation that works out in a demand-like way. Talking intelligibly about evolutionary biology requires as many metaphors as it does to talk intelligible theology.

of particular ways the daylight falls that you'd have to be a Cézanne to begin to annotate them all. And yet it ends. And yet the violet and the slate-grey and the bright gold and the colour of the living blood under the skin of loved faces all go away. It can all be extinguished by a dodgy heart valve. By the thinned wall of one blood vessel in the brain. By a single transcription error in a cell nucleus. Then the lightshow – which we had grown used to, which we thought would last for ever – ceases. My grandmother died recently, four months short of her hundredth birthday, and I remember thinking as I cycled home that night how odd it was that this was the first evening she had missed since February 1911. The whole vast liner strung with coloured bulbs tilts, and goes down into the dark water for ever. It happens every time. Every one of our voyages ends in disaster. Every ship of ours is the *Titanic*.

Lots of atheists seem to be certain, recently, that this ought not to be a problem for believers, because – curl of lip – we all believe we're going to be whisked away to a magic kingdom in the sky instead. Facing the prospect of annihilation squarely is the exclusive achievement of – preen – the brave unbeliever. But I don't know many actual Christians (as opposed to the conjectural idiots of atheist fantasy) who feel this way, or anything like it. Death's reality is a given of human experience, for anyone old enough to have shaken off adolescent delusions of immortality. There it is, the black water, not to be cancelled by declarations, by storytelling, of any kind. Whatever sense belief makes of death, it has to incorporate its self-evident reality, not deny it. And again, in my experience, belief makes the problem harder, not easier. Because there death is, real for us as it is for everyone else, and yet (as with every other outrage of the cruel world) we also have to fit it together somehow with the intermittently felt, constantly transmitted assurance that we are loved. I don't mean to suggest that all believers are in a state of continual anguish about this, but it is a very rare believer who has not had to come to a reckoning with the contradiction involved. On the one hand, the cruel world – the world *made* cruel by seeing it as created – and on the other one, the sensation of being cherished by its creator.

So what to do?

Well, there's self-deception. Because there's *always* self-deception, it's a resource available in every human situation. If you're lucky enough in where you live and when you live and how you live, the problem need not press too hard. (Until, suddenly, it does.) You can then take your benign and comfortable local environment as your picture of what the whole universe is like, for just as there are cosy atheists who mistake their own suburb for a whole dependably surburban cosmos, it must be admitted that there are comfy Christians too. When readily available vaccines mean that your children aren't being blinded by measles[*] as part of evolution's heartlessly efficient arms race between virus and antibodies, it gets

---

[*] Which is a *good* thing, obviously.

easier to relegate suffering to a dim abstraction, and to suppose that your life is in the hands of a divine micro-manager, who tweaks and prunes and coaxes every little event to work out for the best. Squinting, you turn your luck into evidence of favours received. I've seen a church newsletter in which the Almighty is thanked for fixing the minister's car, via a miraculously cheap quote from a garage. But it only takes a little of the cold wind of adversity to blow this stuff away – and only a little thought. For if God was willing to exert Himself over the minister's sparkplugs, but wouldn't get out of bed to stop the Holocaust, what sort of picture would that draw? What sort of loving deity could have the priorities that the cruel world reveals, if the cruel world is an accurate record of His intentions, once you look beyond reality's little gated communities of niceness?

Or, you can argue. You can stipulate for the real existence of suffering, and yet try to find ways in which it means something more bearable than it appears to; something more creditable to God. This brings you to the set of traditional theological answers to the problem, which go under the name of 'theodicy'. Theodicies mostly continue to treat everything that happens as being deliberately intended by God, but acknowledge that a defence is required for some of the – how shall we put this? – less *blatantly friendly* aspects of our environment. Theodicies try to justify God by justifying the cruel world. They vary, but they have one thing in common. None of them quite work. None of them fare well enough against the challenge of experience for them to let us lay the issue to rest, to let us file it under 'solved'. Each tends to find some useful elements of truth to grip on to, but to end up failing, like the miraculous spark-plugs, by drawing a picture of the God of everything which is incompatible with love as we know it to be. And the love of God does have to bear a secure resemblance to what it means for us to love somebody. The nineteenth-century philosopher John Stuart Mill put his finger on something important when he said that he refused to admire any quality in God that he wouldn't admire in one of his friends. He meant it only semi-seriously. It was a way of cutting God down to size; a way of insisting that pious awe shouldn't stop you from making straightforward judgements on anything claimed to be a piece of God's behaviour, like Randolph Churchill stuck in a Yugoslav cave during the Second World War with only a bible to read, and saying, as he waded through Old Testament plagues and tribulations, 'What a shit God is!' In effect, Mill was asserting that the only definitions of goodness that can matter are everyday, familiar human ones. It's a stance which fails to engage with what would be unique to the God of everything, His universal responsibility. It also rules out the significant possibility that there may be forms of goodness which cannot be fully manifested by hungry, squabbling, brief creatures like us. But it has the great advantage of putting *recognition* at the centre of the issue. We really do need to know that 'love', when God does it, does not mean some glacial alien quality, repellently bound up with the calculations of power, which only shares a terminology with our emotion. We really can check an account of the bits of God's behaviour we can see against our own understanding – not looking for a match, but looking for an overlap. There has to be an overlap. The love of the God of everything need not be exhausted by the human definition of love, but it must not contradict it either, if He is to be worth worshipping.

Take a theodicy. For instance, *We suffer because God is refining us*. The element of truth that is being seized on here is that there are virtues which, quite genuinely, can only be developed by endurance. There truly are ways in which we need to experience bad things and things that aren't pleasures in order to have selves which are strongly made, selves of which we can tell ourselves coherent stories. Observably true so far; but the idea that suffering might be being lovingly distributed by God as a form of education cracks open and collapses on the equally observable counter-truth that the bad stuff gets distributed with an utterly un-educational lack of proportion. The ills of the world are not all neatly sized so that we can cope with them. It is not true that we are never tested beyond our power to endure. And where we're overwhelmed by suffering, where we're humiliated and made into victims, it doesn't make us stronger. The opposite effect comes into play – the lesson 'all school-children learn', according to W. H. Auden:

> Those to whom evil is done
> Do evil in return.

Suffering doesn't on the whole ennoble us. Usually it debases and distorts us, turning us more than ever into creatures who want to pay harms back to someone. Checked against the knowledge of schoolchildren, the theodicy fails.

Or there's *We suffer because God has a plan in which our suffering is necessary*, with its suggestion that a vast, wise, cosmic strategy is in play which we can't see from our restricted standpoint. Here the helpful truth is that God, if He's there at all, cannot be confined in time as we are. The God of everything, if you believe in Him, must be the God of all times at once. Accordingly, He cannot be limited to perceiving things in sequence as we do. He must know the whole pleated manifold of history from side to side and back to front and corner to corner, in every direction, including therefore every question about why things happen, and what is going to happen to us, and what it will cumulatively come to mean that it has happened. And it is also necessarily true, if you believe that the universe was created, that it must in a sense have been planned. It must have been inherently intended to be as it is, with a disposition towards complexity, and towards consciousness, and towards the production of beings like us in whom the God of everything seemingly delights. That must have been a possibility built in from the start.* So far,

---

* Not the same thing as saying that there will be handy proof of God's authorship tucked away in the details of astrophysics. I'm talking about what belief says must have been an intention behind

so planned. Yet the criterion of recognisable love then shows that our suffering can't be planned in the justifying way that the theodicy requires. If love is love, it can't manipulate. If love is love, it can't treat those it loves as means to an end, even a beneficial one. Love is love because it sees its loved ones as ends in themselves, not tools or instruments to achieve some further goal. So suffering can't be vindicated by a pay-off elsewhere. Again the quiz-show buzzer for a wrong answer sounds. Fail.

Next? *We suffer as part of a package deal that gives us free will.* Well, this one actually passes the love test, and therefore gives us some purchase on the question of why God might permit human history to take its savage course, but fails at once as a general justification because it offers no help at all with the other kinds of suffering, the kinds that are not caused by human action. Yes, an intervened-in history, a history pestered with angels, would not be fully *our* history; a pruned version of human autonomy, with the scope for evil lessened or removed, would be a falsified autonomy. Yes, a God of everything who loved us would have to behave as love requires, and allow us to belong fully to ourselves, and therefore to be

the universe, not about something you can deduce from the value of the cosmological constant. The latest thinking I've seen suggests that the universe is not, in fact, precisely fine-tuned to support life. It isn't a Goldilocks universe, neither too hot nor too cold but just right; it's a good-enough universe, adequate for us to muddle into being in. As ever, you have to believe, or not, without science deciding the issue for you.

free to do unlimited harm. He would have to stand back helplessly as a parent of an adult child does, thwartedly tender, twisting His hands in anguish as He refuses to pay our drug debts. But what about the rest? What about earthquakes, gangrene, super-novas? You can pull your adult child out of quicksand without threatening their autonomy. Fail. Next? *We suffer, but it doesn't matter, because it's only a moment-ary prelude to heaven.* Dear oh dear; give me strength. A comprehensive and instant fail, this time, because whether or not you believe that heaven is real, this life certainly is, and so is the suffering it contains. You can't deal with the problem by ignoring it. The only useful element here is a hope you can hang on to, that love will outlast trouble; otherwise, it makes the loving God into a practitioner of dodgy cost–benefit analysis, indifferent to the way our lives feel as we live them. It turns Him into a doctor who thinks it's OK to chat and dawdle on the way to the emergency room, because He does have the morphine, and He will get there eventually, when He gets round to it, after an hour or two of our screaming. No; really not. Really not a plausible characterisation of any kind of lover.

The one that comes nearest to working is probably *We suffer because the world is not as God intended it to be*, and indeed, it has a long and distinguished his-tory as a Christian idea that's compatible both with experience and with keeping God's love recognisable. Environment somewhat ramshackle, a bewildering

combination of the glorious and the downright in-
sanitary? Check. Message of love steadily broadcasting
through the pitfalls and razor edges of said environment? Check. God as kind, aghast, sympathetic to
our sorrow? Check. Surely we have a winner. Oh.
Wait. The trouble with this one is that its convincing picture of the state of things requires, in turn,
an explanation of how they got like that. How could
the God of everything, the creator who precedes and
sustains all nature, whose love song summons nature
into existence, produce something defective? And
now the question is just a restatement, in slightly different terms, of the original problem. 'How can God
permit suffering?' has become 'How can God permit a universe that permits suffering?' The problem
doesn't vanish, it merely relocates, it merely moves
back a step.

You can see this happening in the very first version
of the idea, the Hebrew myth of the Fall in the second
chapter of the Book of Genesis. Once, says Genesis,
God planned for human beings to live in immortal
happiness, but then – Adam, Eve, tree, hiss, munch,
whoops, figleaves, goodbye. It wasn't God's fault. It
was down to us, or at least to our representatives Mr
Earth and Mrs Woman (which is what 'Adam' and 'Eve'
mean), manifesting the familiar human capacity to
screw the pooch, to snatch defeat from the jaws of
victory, to mess up a good thing. But that just shifts
the problem. It only moves God from being directly
responsible for the Fall, to being responsible for the

situation that was responsible for the Fall. The cut-out or circuit-breaker Genesis tries to install between God and a derelict creation simply recreates the difficulty. And in any case, Genesis is fatally confused about where HPtFtU comes from. Genesis chapter 2 wants to have it both ways, with the nasty side of our free will both causing the disaster and, somehow, being caused by it as well. We're fallen because of our HPtFtU; we have the HPtFtU because, um, we're fallen.

Not only is this no good to us as history, as almost all Christians know,* it isn't even any use as story. It makes immediate, intuitive emotional sense to see the universe around us as being 'fallen', but then we find

---

* Except for some really stubborn Americans. It would be a kindness, by the way, and a service to history, if you could please rid yourself of the legend that Christians believed a fairy tale about the origin of the world until forced to think otherwise by the triumph of secular science. Substantially everyone in the Judeo-Christian bits of the planet believed the Genesis account until the early nineteenth century, remember, there being till then no organised alternative. The work of reading the geological record, and thereby exploding the Genesis chronology, was for the most part done not by anti-Christian refuseniks but by scientists and philosophers thinking their way onward from starting-points within the religious culture of the time. Once it became clear that truth lay elsewhere than in Genesis, religious opinion on the whole moved with impressive swiftness to accommodate the discovery. In the same way, when the *Origin of Species* was published, most Christians in Britain at least moved with some speed to incorporate evolutionary biology into their catalogue of ordinary facts about the world. Bishop Samuel Wilberforce's resistance to Darwinism was an outlier, untypical. In fact, there's a good case to be made that the ready acceptance of evolution in Britain owed a lot to the great cultural transmission mechanism of the Church of England. If you're glad that Darwin is on the £10 note, hug an Anglican.

we haven't got a Fall. The plausibility and compre-
hensibility of any candidate vision seem to be inversely
related. The easier a picture is to understand of creation's soap-slick escape from God's almighty hands,
the less likely a story it seems to be. We can understand Genesis's sex comedy in a garden setting,
but it doesn't give us much purchase on a process
by which love can beget cholera. At the other end
of the scale, immense abstract effort across the centuries has gone into producing speculative accounts
of means by which good might just conceivably produce evil. This is where the theology of Gnosticism
comes from, with its zillions of finicky little 'emana-
tions' between us and God, all getting grubbier and
grubbier as they approach the (yuck) matter we're
made of. And the complicated diagrams of kabbal-
ism, separating out different aspects of divinity in
order to incestuously recombine them. And for that
matter, the entire 'dialectical' strand in respectable
philosophy, from Mr Plotinus through to Mr He-
gel and Mr Marx, in which change happens through
the invocation and integration of opposites. But the
obscurity of these unverifiable guesses at God's absolutely obscure operations takes us further and further
away from the emotions that motivated them. Why is
the world unjust? Why does my brilliant friend have
a brain tumour? Why is my child disabled? Why is my
disabled child dying in pain and confusion before her
fifth birthday, despite the best that medicine can do?
I never heard of anyone being comforted by Kabbala,

or by ingenious secret truths, or by the negation of negation – or even feeling that they had been substantially answered by these things. You get more for your money, emotionally speaking, if you just howl, and kick as hard as you can at the imagined ankles of the God of everything, for it is one of His functions, and one of the ways in which He's parent-like, to be the indestructible target for our rage and sorrow, still there, still loving, whatever we say to Him. The element of useful truth in this last and best of theodicies is the reminder it contains that the creation is not the same as the creator. He may sustain it all, He may be its bright backing, He may be as near to us at every moment as our neck-veins: but it is not Him, it is not-Him, it is in some utterly mysterious sense what happens where He isn't. To anyone inclined to think, in a happy wafty muddly way, that nature *is* God, nature replies: have a cup of pus, Mystic Boy.

And that's about the end of what argument can do for us.

How, then, *do* we deal with suffering? How do we resolve the contradiction between cruel world and loving God? The short answer is that we don't. We don't even try to, mostly. Most Christian believers don't spend their time and their emotional energy stuck at this point of contradiction. For most of us, worrying about it turns out to have been a phase in the early history of our belief. The question of suffering proves to be one of those questions which is replaced by other questions, rather than being answered. We move on from it, without abolishing the mystery, or seeing clear conceptual ground under our feet. Cataclysmic experiences *can* pitch us back into it of course, but mostly they don't. Even in bad times we usually don't go back there. We take the cruelties of the world as a given, as the known and familiar data of experience, and instead of anguishing about why the world is as it is, we look for comfort in coping with it as it is. We don't ask for a creator who can explain Himself. We ask for a friend in time of grief, a true judge in time of perplexity, a wider hope than we can manage in time of despair. If your child is dying, there is no reason that can ease your sorrow. Even if, impossibly, some true and sufficient explanation could be given you, it wouldn't help, any more than the inadequate and defective explanations help you, whether they are picture-book simple or inscrutably contorted. The only comfort that can do anything – and probably the most it can do is help you to endure, or if you cannot endure to fail and fold without wholly hating yourself – is the comfort of feeling yourself loved. Given the cruel world, it's the love song we need, to help us bear what we must; and, if we can, to go on loving.

We don't forget, mind. It doesn't escape us that there seems to be something wrong with any picture in which God's in His heaven and all's well with the world. We still know that if He can help us and He doesn't, He isn't worth worshipping; and that if He doesn't help us because He can't, there must be something weirdly limited about the way He's the God of everything. The

impasse is still there. It's just that we're not in the jaws
of it. We're not being actively gripped and chewed by it.
Our feelings have moved on elsewhere. Because there
is a long answer, too, to the question of suffering; a
specifically Christian perception of what God is, which
helps us move on.

I don't honestly know how Jews and Muslims cope
on this point, given that both Judaism and Islam basically do announce that God's in His heaven, etc. etc.
Presumably the orthopraxy of the other two monotheisms – all the detailed right-doing they ask for –
creates a kind of emotional buffer. They don't ask their
believers to do the right thing because it will necessarily make them prosper, after all: the deal is much
more stoical than that. Righteousness is righteousness,
in Judaism and Islam, irrespective of how it works out
for you personally. You do the right thing because it's
the right thing. If you flourish, great; if you don't, I
imagine you can at least hold on to the deep grooves of
holy habit, carved into your life over and over by repetition, a repetition which itself must feel like a kind of
evidence that the cosmos is benign. The stars may fall,
the plague may come, but the five daily prayers still roll
around. Maybe you pray them with extra fervour then,
because they represent your life's remaining pieces of
dignity and order.

Christians too, of course, draw consolation from the
patterns faith makes as it repeats in time. For us too
there's an important wisdom in not leading a life
whose only measure is the impulse of the moment. But

our main comfort in the face of unjustifiable suffering is very different. It's not an investment in order we're asked to make; it's a gamble on change. Our hope is not in time cycling on predictably and benevolently under an almighty hand. Our hope is in time interrupted, disrupted, abruptly altering from moment to moment. We *don't* say that God's in His heaven and all's well with the world; not deep down. We say: all is not well with the world, but at least God is here in it, with us. We don't have an argument that solves the problem of the cruel world, but we have a story.

When I pray, I am not praying to a philosophically complicated absentee creator. When I manage to pay attention to the continual love song, I am not trying to envisage the impossible-to-imagine domain beyond the universe. I do not picture kings, thrones, crystal pavements, or any of the possible cosmological updat- ings of these things. I look across, not up; I look into the world, not out or away. When I pray I see a face, a human face among other human faces. It is a face in an angry crowd, a crowd engorged by the confid- ence that it is doing the right thing, that it is being virtuous. The man in the middle of the crowd does not look virtuous. He looks tired and frightened and battered by the passions around him. But he is the crowd's focus and centre. The centre of everything, in fact, because if you are a Christian you do not believe that the characteristic action of the God of everything is to mould the course of the universe powerfully from afar. For a Christian, the most essential thing

God does in time, in all of human history, is to be
that man in the crowd; a man under arrest, and on
his way to our common catastrophe.

5

Yeshua

Imagine a man, then.[*] It's the man from the crowd, but he hasn't arrived there yet. Imagine a man in whom the overwhelming, all-at-once perspective of the God of everything is not a momentary glimpse from which he rebounds, reeling, but a continual presence which in him is somehow adapted to the scale of the human mind, so that for him, uniquely, the shining is not other but self. So that he sees the world at every moment with the thwarted tenderness of its creator. So that he *is* that creator, not his spokesman or his representative or his ambassador, but the creator him- or her- or itself, no longer thwarted but also no longer immune. He's the creator in the midst of the thing made, in the place which the shining backs and sustains but where it does not seem to reach to act, judging by what goes on in here; where it or she or he will be subject like the rest of us to the logic of biology, and the logic of human politics, and the logics of fear and loss and uncertainty.

---

[*] I say 'imagine' and I mean imagine. This is the story we have instead of an argument, and it is important that it *is* a story, making a story-like sense, and having a story's chance to move us, with human stuff organised into a tellable pattern in time. But while a story is not the same thing as a lie, there are stories and stories. If you'll hang on till I've (re)told this one, I undertake to bring some critical rigour to bear in the next chapter on the question of just what kind of story it is.

What does he look like? No idea. No one is ever going to write down a description. He's a male Jew in first-century Palestine, so he's probably bearded, a bit smelly by modern standards, and quite short. He may well have bad or missing teeth. He is in his early thirties in an age of hard labour and rudimentary medicine, when the average life expectancy is forty-something, so he may well be rather worn out and middle-aged. But we don't know. And it really doesn't matter. He looks like us, for a value of 'us' which includes the entire human race. We have faces and bodies; he has a face and a body. He is as human as we are, but if you meet him, you are also meeting the being responsible for the universe. He has no halo. He does not glow in the dark. Special lighting effects do not announce his presence. If you cut him he bleeds. His name is Yeshua, later to be Latinised as 'Jesus'. And what he has come for? To say some things; to do some things.

The place he has come to (the place he has been born into) is a province of the empire that controls pretty much the whole known world. The empire has owned it for two generations, but it has not been independent for much longer. Before this empire there was another one, and another one before that. The province is not specially important, or specially rich. It has no famous sights. The only city is a huddle of yellow stone on a desert hilltop. But it is unusual. It is the only place in the world, so far, which is populated by worshippers of the God of everything. You can find scatterings of them elsewhere but this is the single place in which they are the majority, the natives. This is where their history happened. This is where they have worked their way from thinking that their God is the most important god, to thinking that He is the only God for them, to thinking that He is the only God there is. One-ness, singleness, commands their imaginations. Just as their god is The God, their land is The Land, and their city is The City.

The imperial authorities, seeing the peculiarity of the place, try to be tactful. They rule as much as possible at arm's length, using the local potentates left over from the previous empire as their proxies. They keep the garrisons out of sight as much as they can. They police with a light touch. But the inhabitants hate the empire anyway. They insist on perceiving even the tactful version of imperial rule as a grotesque violation. For them, the usual deal the empire offers – obey, pay our taxes, and you're welcome to pour your culture into the vast blend of ours – doesn't work. For them, it has no upside. They don't want the one God found a junior spot among the gods of Dental Health, Matching Curtains and Being Well Endowed. They don't want Him blended. Blending would be adulteration. Or, in fact, adultery. Their prophets have told them over and over again how unfaithful they are, what a bunch of wandering-eyed wife-swappers and sluts they are in relation to their ever-committed God, and by now the metaphor has settled in, to the point that they reflexively think of worshipping any other god as being promiscuous, and conversely of literal promiscuity as having a dimension of sacrilege or existential betrayal to it. So puritanism mixes with ethical outrage when they look at – when they whisper about – the cruel, easygoing grossness of the empire. They don't want any of that disgusting stuff the occupiers do, where the men go to the gym and cover themselves in olive oil and walk around nearly naked; or where they take their big muscles to the theatre, and fight each other till someone dies, while everyone laughs and cheers and throws peanuts.

This is not how the world is supposed to be. The world is supposed to be dignified, righteous, law-governed. For though the occupiers have laws, they are mere human contrivances; their own laws, they believe, are *real* laws, given directly by God on a mountaintop. A copy stands in the meeting-house in every village and town where the men get together on Saturday to pray and argue, in the place of honour where the rest of the empire would put a statue of Being Well Endowed in his posing pouch. The law is sacred. It is the embodiment of God's intentions in the world. It lays out the demanding but achievable pattern for a life of virtue. It tells you what to eat and what to wear and how to behave, to please God. It tells you the rules for getting back into good standing with Him, if you have been stained by the chances and mishaps of life, or by your own bad behaviour. (Usually you do it by sacrificing something, in the city, in the one temple which is The Temple.) Thanks to the adultery metaphor, these rules feel a lot like recipes for regaining purity. But there's a huge collective impurity the law cannot tell them how to remove: the occupation itself. The empire and its filthy gods encroach. Tourists wander into holy places, chattering and laughing. The empire's money with its blasphemous pictures has to be used for buying innocent, ordinary bread. It's as if the people of the province are being kept forcibly dirty, all the time. Somehow, they think, the favour of God has been forfeited. For some reason, they are being punished.

What they want is what the empire by definition will not give them: their separateness, their independence. They want the country their law implies, the kingdom of their own that they used to have, long ago, before the empires. In memory it has grown from a hardscrabble patch of rocks and olive trees into something verging on a different state of being. The kingdom has started to represent righteousness itself, the state (in both senses of the word) in which God's people live in accord with Him again. It has become the focus of their longing. But a longing that cannot be acted upon. The occupiers are much too strong. Even tucked away in their barracks, the people know they are there, enormous brawny thugs with bare knees, backed up by superb organisation, matchless military technology, the wealth of the whole world.

So the province simmers. As you would expect, the young men find a particular testosterone-fuelled humiliation in their powerlessness. As you would expect, the burdens of the laws of purity fall with particular weight on the young women. As you would expect, collaborators are hated. As you would expect, so are prostitutes, especially if they have anything to do with the army camps. As you would expect, the high officials of the one God's one temple perform a difficult balancing act, trying to keep the people happy, trying to keep the occupiers sweet so they don't take away even more of the province's limited autonomy. Low-level terrorism flourishes, followed by example-setting public executions. An ever-changing selection of pious groups offer ever-changing prescriptions for getting back God's approval. Preachers and would-be prophets are everywhere, prominent for a season and then gone. Some people say the rules of purity should be even stricter. Some people say you should abandon everything and go into the clean desert. Some people say you need to be washed in the province's one river. A lot of people think that the world will end soon; fear it will end soon; hope it will end soon, because then a more than human justice may put things right. All the time, there are whispered rumours of someone, somewhere, claiming the kingship and starting the holy war to get the kingdom back. It never seems to be true, but every fanatic up in the hills knows the role is waiting to be filled. The religion has made a space for this figure, the king-who-is-to-come, the man whom the God of everything will choose to lead the uprising. He is called *moshiakh*, 'the anointed one', after the holy oil that kings wear. In Greek, where oil for hair is *chrism*, his title translates as *christos*. But it's a no-show so far for Mr Royal Oil. In summer the tension gets specially bad; and also at festivals, which are supposed to celebrate things being right, and make it feel much worse that they aren't. The soldiers are jumpy and resentful too. They don't like it here. The fleshpots of the exotic East it isn't. The locals are loons. Any moment, some teenage boy may try to stab you with a kitchen knife, and you can't tell if the girls are babes because they're all covered up. It's a grim little armpit of a posting. Say the wrong thing, eat the wrong thing, touch the wrong thing – any little thing can kick off a riot.

Into this setting comes Yeshua, with the love song to all that is ringing continually in him, and he says: don't be careful.

He certainly isn't careful himself. He and his friends come wandering into town on the holy Saturday when you're not supposed to work or to travel, or to do anything much, and they're chewing and laughing, they're picnicking in the street as they stroll along. Challenged, he says (with his mouth full) that the rules are for the people, not the people for the rules. When crowds gather, to check out this new source of entertainment or outrage, to see if he's conducting himself like a teacher or a prophet or just possibly like a guerrillero looking for recruits – when the crowds gather, he sits them down in the sheep pasture, and he says: behave as if you never had to be afraid of consequences. Behave as if nothing you gave away could ever make you poorer, because you can never run out of what you give. Behave as if this one day we're in

115

now were the whole of time, and you didn't have to hold anything back, or to plot and scheme about tomorrow. Don't try to grip your life with tight, anxious hands. Unclench those fingers. Let it go. If someone asks for your help, give them more than they've asked for. If someone hits out at you, let them. Don't retaliate. Be the place the violence ends. Because you've got it wrong about virtue. It isn't something built up from a thousand careful, carefully measured acts. It comes, when it comes, in a rush; it comes from behaving, so far as you can, like God Himself, who makes and makes and loves and loves and is never the less for it. God doesn't want your careful virtue, He wants your reckless generosity. Try to keep what you have, and you'll lose even that. Give it away, and you'll get back more than you bargain for; more than bargaining could ever get you. By the way, you were wanting a king? Look at that flower over there by the wall. More beautiful than any royal robe, don't you think? Better than silks; and it comes bursting out of the ground all by itself, free and gratis. It won't last? Nothing lasts; nothing but God.

He isn't a relativist, though. Far from it. He doesn't think you should relax and do what you like, and it won't really matter what. He believes in good and evil all right, to a drastic degree. He has a vivid, horrified sense of the HPtFtU, in all its elaborate self-deceiving semi-oblivious encrustedness, and he talks as if it overshadowed huge swathes of human activity, including the human activities that humans tend to be

116

proud of. Whenever anyone asks him about the law, he usually ups the ante; he amps the law up towards a perfectionist impossibility, in which anger is forbidden as well as murder, in which desire can be as much of a betrayal as adultery – in which internal states of being that apparently don't hurt (or even affect) anyone else weigh as heavily with God as external acts. Sometimes he seems to be a kind of radical pessimist about human nature. Who are you calling good? he says, when someone makes the mistake of addressing him with ordinary social politeness as 'good man'. No one is good but God. He talks as if virtue is almost unachievable, yet still compulsory. Rather than being a menu of demands that all can satisfy, for him it seems to be something that it would take feats of absurd unlikelihood to accomplish, rents or openings or transformations in the order of nature, so that camels can climb through needles' eyes. He talks a lot about fire sometimes, about burning. He seems to think a change is required in us as complete as the change that comes when chaff is set blazing after the harvest, and the fields billow with flame. We must all be 'salted with fire', he says. He can be frightening, indeed he can. He says it would be worth chopping off bits of yourself – eyes, hands – if it would rid you of what separates you from God. Yet he is an optimistic pessimist. Come *on*, says somebody. How could anybody *ever* stand right with God, if it were as hard as you say? With God, everything is possible, he says.

He annoys people when he talks like this. Because

the implication of his perfectionism is that everybody is guilty; and if everybody is guilty, nobody gets to congratulate themselves, and murderers and adulterers cannot be shunned. If what he says is right, then those are only people in whom the universal HPtFtU has taken a particular turn, has been indulged in particular ways. They are not outcasts, they do not belong in a category of unclean persons that the clean rest of us can hold at arm's length. Yeshua insists that being unclean is not a temporary violation of the proper state of things. It is the normal human condition. Yet he seems weirdly unbothered about sex. Except to make it clear that it falls under the umbrella of his perfectionism, he hardly has a thing to say about it. He expresses no opinions whatsoever about homosexuality, abortion, promiscuity, contraception, clerical celibacy, virginity at marriage, modest dress, non-procreative sex, masturbation, gay marriage, or how far you should go on a first date. He appears to be opposed to divorce on the pro-feminist grounds that it cuts women off without economic support. (In his world, men can divorce women but not the other way round.) He does not denounce anything. He does not seem to be disgusted by anybody, anybody at all. It is as if, shockingly, what we do in bed is not specially important to him. As if it just does not constitute for him a particularly prominent and anxious category of human behaviour. Whether he has any passions of his own, and what kind, and who for, no one has been interested in telling us, any more than they have bothered to say what he looks like.*

On the other hand, he has a *lot* to say about self-righteousness, which he compares, not very tactfully, to a grave that looks neat and well cared for up top but is heaving with 'corruption' down below. Maggots, basically. And the point of this repulsive image is not just that the inside and outside of a self-righteous person don't match, that there's a hypocritical contradiction between the claim to virtue and the actual content of a human personality: it's also that, for him, being sure you're righteous, standing on your dignity as a virtuous person, comes precious close to being dead. If you won't hear the bad news about yourself, you can't know yourself. You condemn yourself to the maintenance of an exhausting illusion, a false front to your self which keeps out doubt and with it hope, change, nourishment, breath, life. If you won't hear the bad news, you can't begin to hear the good news about yourself either. And you'll do harm. You'll be pumped up with the false confidence of virtue, and you'll think it gives you a licence, and a large share of all the cruelties in the world will follow, for evil done knowingly is rather rare compared to the evil done by people who're sure that they themselves are good, and that evil is hatefully concentrated in some other person; some other person

---

* For the question of whether, instead, his sex life has been brutally excised from the documents by a body-hating church – again, please wait for the next chapter. Go on, you can hold out. Take a deep breath.

who makes your flesh creep because they have become exactly as unbearable, as creepy, as disgusting, as you fear the mess would be beneath your own mask of virtue, if you ever dared to look at it.

He arrives in a town just as a public execution is about to take place. The criminal is a woman 'taken in adultery', which could mean that she's been caught having literal sex with someone other than her husband. But it could also mean that she smiles at soldiers when she serves wine to them, or that she's been seen chatting at the well with a boy who is neither her brother nor her cousin; or it could mean that she works in the brothel the town is ashamed it possesses, and has been servicing five burghers a night for a decade. One way or another she has concentrated in herself the town's fear and alarm about desire. And the good people have gathered to punish her. They already have in their hands the rocks the law stipulates, neither too small nor too big, which will crack her bones and mash out of her flesh the disturbance of her desirability. Yeshua intervenes, which is not necessarily a very sensible thing to do, when virtue is breathing fast and looking forward to this kind of treat. He asks what she's done. They tell him. Oh, he says. Well then, the one of you who's never wanted anything bad had better throw the first stone. And he raises his eyebrows and waits, and something in the gaze of his ordinary eyes makes the good people shuffle where they stand. There's a pause. Perhaps it helps that his friends have walked into town with him, equally dusty from the road, and that among the rag-tag of his followers, male and female, who're hanging back to see what he does, there are some quite large and burly men. But anyway there's the hollow *klok* and *klok* and *klok* of stones dropping onto the ground, and the executioners slink away, and in a moment or two only the executee is left there with Yeshua and his friends. She is weeping. He helps her to stand up.

This kind of thing does not make him popular, and nor does his persistent refusal to show any respect for people's sense of their own spiritual accomplishments, which comes out in his bizarre attitude to the question of where he has dinner each night. The usual custom, when a preacher or a would-be prophet is doing well out on the circuit, is for him to accept an invite from a pious local dignitary: someone upstanding, a pillar of the meeting-house, a bit of a connoisseur of the finer points of the law, who will feed the rising star, and in return get a private performance of whatever the new thing is he's offering, as after-dinner entertainment. But Yeshua keeps ignoring the invitations and picking the night's host for himself, from out of the crowd – again and again unerringly settling on some really unrespectable citizen, someone like a wineshop owner the pious would ignore in the street, or on an out-and-out public enemy, like a tax-farmer for the empire. And when, for a change, he does accept a meal from the upright, he has a way of being casually, intimately offensive to his host. So tell me, teacher – says a solid citizen as the remains of the baked eggplant are cleared away – what must I do to be saved? Yeshua's gaze slides across the tapestries, the silver bowls for washing guests' feet, the candlestick blessed by the Chief Priest of the temple himself. I'd get rid of this lot for a start, he says.

People bristle. The news about him gets around. He starts to pick up hecklers, to be drawn into staged conversations designed to get him into trouble or to make him declare himself unambiguously for one of the factions. He arrives in new towns and anti-welcoming committees greet him. Take the crazy talk somewhere else, they say. But it isn't just strangers who think he's making a fool of himself. His own family think so too. They are embarrassed by him, and beginning to be frightened for him as well, correctly seeing that if he goes on like this, he is cruising for a bruising. One day when he's preaching in a house, and the alleyway outside is blocked solid with interested onlookers, his mother and his brothers and sisters turn up in a body to retrieve him. They can't force their way through the crush, so they send in a message: tell him his family have come to take him home, tell him his mother's here and very upset, tell him it's time to stop all this nonsense. But he won't go. He won't even come out to talk to them. Instead he weaves their message straight into what he's saying. Mother? Brother? Sister? What are those? What good does it do if we only love those who love us back? God wants more than kin loving kin. He wants more than the natural bonds. He wants more than biology. He wants our love to do more than run around the tight circle of our self-interest; more, even, than that it should run around the wider circle of our altruism, if altruism means we get some kind of round-about payback for love in the end. God, he says, wants us to love wildly and without calculation. God wants us to love people we don't even like; people we hate; people who hate us. He says this, and he looks away from the familiar faces who're bobbing up and down behind the wall of shoulders in the doorway, calling to him, trying to be heard. He isn't going with them. His brothers, his sisters, his mother start the long walk home, defeated.

By the way, he says. The law is not enough, either. It may be necessary, but it is not sufficient. That book in the place of honour in the meeting-house is a gift from the one God, but it is not His only gift; it is not the whole pattern of what He wants from us; it does not capture, perfect and entire, His whole intentions towards us. God knows that we need justice, without which no human city can stand. There must be rule by rules, or force will tear down every wall. Since blood will be shed no matter what, humans being humans, better that it should be shed to try to protect the weak from the strong, to guard the widow and the orphan and the traveller on the road, to settle quarrels without massacres. Innocence and guilt must be portioned out. Punishments must be assigned. Judgements must be made. Our nature requires it. But God's nature doesn't. The law is needful for us, not for Him. God is not in the game of harnessing fear and anger, and trying to turn them into fairness. God does not need to struggle to get from the shouting and the screaming and the sword in the night to the calm room where a judge is doing their best to see what somebody deserves. The law says that everyone should get what they deserve, but God already knows what we deserve with terrible precision, and He wants us to have more than that. He sees that we need to do justice to each other, but he wants to give us mercy. He wants deserving to be overflooded by love. So, if you want to live in accord with Him, you can't do it just by being law-abiding. You have to try, again, to be like Him, and to do what He does. He doesn't wait for us to come to Him where He is, out there beyond the need for the law; He comes to us, right now, where we live in the grip of our necessities, to bring us the rest of His gift, to complete the work the law began.

And yet, though Yeshua is telling people to discard the dream of perfect law, he somehow still wants the kingdom anyway. He talks about the kingdom all the time, every day, almost every hour, as much as any of the threadbare bandits in the hills who tell themselves they'll be sitting on silk cushions in the city when the *christos* comes. Yes, the kingdom is coming, he says. But in his mouth the great object of the province's yearning for a century and more turns . . . elusive. When he talks about it, it skips from analogy to analogy, keeping all its power as heart's desire and humiliation's remedy, but sliding ever onward, impossible to pin down as a political plan. Yeshua's kingdom apparently exists in ever-changing resemblances. He does not say what it *is*, only what it is like. It's like a tiny seed. It's like a big tree. Like something inside you. Like a pearl you'd give everything to possess. Like wheat growing among weeds. Like the camel climbing through the needle's eye. Like the way the world looks to children. Like a servant making good use of the master's money. Like getting a day's pay for an hour's work. Like a crooked magistrate, who has fixed the case in your favour. Like a narrow gate, a difficult road, a lamp on a stand. Like a wedding party. Like a wedding party where all the original guests have been disinvited and replaced by random passers-by. Like yeast in dough. Like a treasure, like a harvest, like a door that opens whenever you knock. Or like a door you have to bang on for hours in the middle of the night until a grumpy neighbour wakes up and lends you a loaf. The kingdom is – whatever all those likenesses have in common. The kingdom, he seems to be saying, is something that can only be glimpsed in comparisons, because the world contains no actual example of it. And yet the world glints and winks and shines everywhere with the possibility of it. Which is not exactly what you'd call a manifesto.

Things get strange sometimes in the same way when he tells stories. He likes to do this; it's his favourite way of teaching. And he doesn't mean to be mysterious, you can tell. He doesn't mind playing language games when people are trying to trap him into saying something out-and-out arrestable, but the idea is always to be understood. He is a bit sarcastic to his friends when they suggest that he is talking in a secret code, for insiders only. Nothing is hidden except to be revealed, he says. The stories are always about homely, everyday things. They're about sheep, vineyards, money, weddings, bosses and servants, parents and children. And mostly they're perfectly easy to follow, like the story of the rude son who says Fuck off Dad and pulls the blanket over his head when his father tries to call him for work, but arrives in the field at mid-morning with a grunt of apology, while his smoothy-smoothy brother is all Yes Dad, No Dad, but never turns up at all. Or the story of the foreigner who helps the guy who's been mugged. Or the story of the tenants who kill the landlord's son. But then you'll get a story which is just baffling; and not because it is making some profound but hard-to-understand statement, or because it is doing the Zen thing of deliberately invoking an impossibility to jump you into an altered state. These are baffling because they seem to have several different layers of meaning going on at once which don't square up with each other. Wait wait wait, you want to say – so the fellow who wants to be king represents God? But then who is it he's applying to for the royal powers? and who are the people who accuse him of injustice supposed to be? Sorry, what? It's as if when Yeshua talks we're hearing something big and obvious being translated into a form which won't quite hold it. Or, worse, there are stories that seem quite clear, but where the homely details start to seem odder and odder, less and less familiar, the more you think about them.

Say you have a hundred sheep, says Yeshua. And you lose one. Wouldn't you drop everything, wouldn't you leave the remaining ninety-nine, and go in search of the missing one, never resting till it was found? That's what God is like, in search of us. Oh, I see, you say. Yes. But then, after a minute: Er, hello? Er, mister? No. No; not unless you *lock up the ninety-nine other sheep* in a sheepfold first, so you don't lose them too. Because, you know, sheep wander off. And because, you know, you'd want to keep as many of them as possible. That would be your sheep-maximising strategy. That would be, kind of, the point of being a shepherd. You do know, right, that ninety-nine is a bigger number than one? You have actually *seen* sheep, right? And then the same implicitly weird – weird verging on inhuman – thing happens when he tells a story about a woman who has ten coins, loses one, and finds it again. He doesn't seem even to notice the nine coins she still has left. The losing and the getting back are all that stand out to him. He doesn't seem to understand ownership. It's as if someone is speaking for whom loss, and making good on it, is so urgent, so prominent in the world, that they scarcely have any attention left over for possession. What matters is that what is lost should be found, what is broken should be made whole.

Lost people arouse his particular tenderness. In all their varieties. People whose bodies or minds don't work properly. People especially mangled by the HPtFtU. People who one way or another fall foul of the purity rules, whether it's their own doing or not. People who live beyond the usual bounds of sympathy, because they are ugly, or frightening, or boring, or incomprehensible, or dangerous. People who are not people like us, whoever 'we' happen to be; people who are not the right kind of people, whatever that is being defined as. In theory he has come to help the lost sheep among the God-fearers, the lost sheep of Israel – that's what he says – but in practice, over and over again, he gives his whole attention to whoever he meets, including a multitude of foreigners, and members of the occupying army. The lack of limit in what he asks of people, the limitlessness of what he wants for people, washes away the difference between insiders and outsiders. He is never recorded as saying no to anyone. Anyone can claim his time, if they can find a way to him through the crowd, and when someone does, whatever their reason is, he speaks to them as if the dust and the noise and the reaching hands had receded and nothing else were going on in the wide world but he and they talking. All his conversations seem to be personal. Even in argument, even practising neat word-judo on a heckler with an agenda, he appears to be fully focused on the particular individual in front of him. When he offends a rich person by advising them to dump their possessions, he does not say it to push them away; it is his real prescription for what afflicts them, and when they do not take his remedy he is sorry, if unsurprised. He seems to know the names of strangers without asking. He knows things about their histories too. One by one, as they get their moment with him, they are each vividly, substantially present to him. They matter. They matter in themselves. They are not means to an end. He is not like a politician in a democracy, who wants to convert instances of individual liking into a bloc of votes; or a war leader, who wants charisma to win him a devoted army; or a lawgiver, like Moses or Muhammad, who is thinking in terms of the health of the group. It is not a good day for him when he wins lots of new followers, or a bad day for him when he doesn't. Yeshua's sense of people is not additive. More is not better. Each person in front of him is, for that moment, the one missing sheep.

And he is never disgusted. He never says that anything – anyone – is too dirty to be touched. That anyone is too lost to be found. Even in situations where there seem to be no grounds for human hope, he will not agree that hope is gone beyond recall. Wreckage may be written into the logic of the world, but he will not agree that it is all there is. He says, more can be mended than you fear. Far more can be mended than you know.

He tells another story. A father has two sons. One is a steady type, content to work away on the farm, but the younger one is all flash and leather trousers, and he persuades his dad to let him have his share of the inheritance up front, so he can have fun fun fun with

it. Which he does, away in the big city, draining the
bucket of fun deeper and deeper, sleazier and sleazier,
down into the sump of fun where the fun is really not
that much fun any more, but still kind of compelling,
so you keep on doing it, despite many resolutions to
stop, because if you do stop you'll let yourself see what
you're losing; right down to the last few extraordin-
arily disgusting mouthfuls, during which the younger
son does things he can't bear to even name. Until finally the bucket is empty, and there's nothing left but
the bitter knowledge of waste, and the younger son is
alone and penniless and ruined, in the gutter of the
big city: and he wants to creep back home, because
that's all that's left. But he doesn't know whether home
is even there for him now, and he doesn't really see
why it should be; after all, it was home he traded in for
the fun fun fun, it was his stake in home he was burning up, it was home he was choosing against all that
time. So as he makes the long walk in the ridiculous
rags of his party-wear, clothes not made for dusty noon
on the road, with his blisters oozing and the sour stink
of old vomit lingering, he rehearses the speech he's
going to make when he gets there: Dad, I know I've
already had all I deserve from you, and then some, and
I don't deserve to be your son, but can I just come back
as a farmhand, and sleep in the barn? But when he's
stumbling down the last hill, before he's even reached
the farm gate, he sees a figure on the road running
to meet him, and it's his father, weeping and laughing
and waving his arms in the air. Dad, he says, I – but

his father ignores the speech; he just kisses him, smelly scarecrow that he is, and hugs him as if he's never going to let go again. This is my son, he shouts, this is my son who was lost and is found. Heat the bathwater! Start cooking a feast! Invite all the neighbours over!

That's not the end of the story, though. It doesn't stop on this moment of pure rejoicing. Because the older brother is there too. He comes in from another day of sober, sensible work to ask what all the commotion is, and when he finds out, he's cautious, and more than a little bit pissed off, as we would be if we responded to the story with our everyday self-protection and scepticism in place. Yeah? the older brother's sour face says – all very touching, but there's only my half of the farm left, and how do you know, Dad, as you wipe the tears out of your beard, that Mr Party Animal here has actually changed? Maybe he's just skint. Also, when did I ever get a feast for staying put and doing what I was supposed to, all along? Not fair.

At which point, the set-up of the story stops making sense, just like the lost sheep did; or rather, it drops away, all the homely talk of farms and brothers, because this is about something else, a love that deliberately does not protect itself, a love that is radically unprotected on purpose, and is never going to stop to ask whether the younger son, like many junkies briefly boomeranging back to the nest, will tomorrow steal the silver spoons and the digital camera and be off again to the fun-bucket. A love that does not come naturally in a world of finite farms, and real inheritances, and exhaustible parents; a love which therefore can only be *like* a father running across the fields to kiss his ruined child. But a love we might need anyway, if we're to get beyond deserving. Yeshua tells the story with the bad boy's viewpoint first, and then the brother's, so that those who hear it must become both of them, so that we can recognise ourselves in both of them. Which we do, if we're honest in the way Yeshua recommends. In every life, we have times when we play both parts. We ruin, and we build. We're chaotic, and we're the anxious maintainers of a little bit of order in the face of chaos. We could only join the older brother in asking for fairness, nothing but fairness, if we didn't see ourselves at all in the lost boy. Since we find ourselves in him as well, we too will need, at times, something far less cautious than justice. We too will need sometimes to be met on the road by a love that never shudders at the state we're in, never hesitates to check what it can bear, but only cries: this is my son, who was lost and is found.

How, though? How can an unlimited love be applied in a world of limits? To begin with, as he goes about the province, Yeshua seems to be trying to do it physically. What do you want me to do for you, he asks the people he speaks to, and very often the answer is, heal me; make me better from the diseases that this time and place in human history cannot cure. Leprosy, epilepsy, paralysis, schizophrenia. All the accidents of a biology which palpably is not safe, is not designed, is not secured from harm by the love that backs the uni-

verse. And Yeshua does what he is asked to. He licks
his fingers and makes a paste of mud and spit, he lays
his hands on twitching stick-limbs and the nubs where
hands used to be and the sides of heads which are
canisters of unbearable noise or skittering electricity;
and where he does so, without any fuss or visible fire-
works, the patient shining that precedes all particular
things is somehow enabled, just this once, just at this
particular moment, on a tiny scale, very locally, to seep
through from the brightness beyond into the here and
now, into what is, and to remake it as love would have
it be. Impossibilities occur. Blind eyes suddenly see.
Severed nerve cells reconnect. Legs straighten, infec-
tions recede, pain fades, horrified minds quieten. Up
you get, says Yeshua. Go, get up, live, be in motion, be
about your business, be the mended version of yourself. Perhaps this momentary suspension of the laws
of the universe can happen because the maker of all
things is now no longer outside them, impartially sustaining them, holding everything but touching nothing
in particular. Now, instead, the maker is within as well,
and he has hands that can reach, he has a local address in space and time from which to act. But now,
by the same token, he cannot be everywhere at once.
He has only two hands, one voice. He can only touch
the people who are within the reach of his hands, as
he travels at foot speed or fishing-boat speed around
the province. And he himself, existing in the domain
of limits, has limits too. Healing people exhausts him;
it makes him sway on his feet. Day after day ends with

him helplessly asking his friends to get him away, and they carry him off in a boat, or up into the hills, just so he can sleep, leaving behind the vast total of the world's suffering almost unaltered, only the tiniest inroads made into it, only an infinitesimal fraction of it eased. One man doing miracles in West Asia doesn't even move the leprosy statistics. The cruelty of the cruel world reproduces itself far faster than his slow hands can move. He brings sight to blind eyes, and all the causes of blindness rage on. He interrupts one stoning, and that very week twenty other stonings proceed without a hitch.

He can't mend the world's sorrows this way – weep though he does, berate himself though he does, say yes though he does to every request. The healing of damaged bodies can only be a sign of what he's truly come to do. His business is with the human heart in the metaphorical sense, not with the clenching muscle in our chests. He's here to mend the HPtFtU, not to cure diseases. (And yes, he knows the difference. The idea that disease *is* a sin, or at least a consequence of one, is very popular in the province, and Yeshua takes care to disagree whenever he comes across it.) That's what he means by the camel skipping through the needle's eye, by the lost sheep being found, by the ruined boy coming home. His promise is that the grief we ourselves cause can be mended. How, though? Isn't that even more impossible? Two thousand years later, we can do something about a lot of the diseases that were incurable when Yeshua came, and our knowledge increases year by year, reducing pain far more effectively than isolated miracles could. But how, in a world of consequences, can we possibly be rid of the consequences of our own cruelties and failures – especially when Yeshua is insisting we take ourselves so ferociously seriously? The consequences of the HPtFtU ramify out in time from moments we cannot retrieve. Our past is past, definitively out of reach. The child you neglected grew up into the adult who will always be shaped, in part, by the neglect. The effort you failed to put into your first marriage left your ex-partner with scar tissue that is now part of him. The nervous teenager you talked into trying skunk in Amsterdam in 1997, the one who had the psychotic reaction to it, is still living at home with her parents, still frightened, still unquiet in mind. None of it can be unpicked, revised, done over again. So how can the weight of it, which Yeshua insists we should feel as the first step towards hope, possibly be lifted off us?

The existing religion of the God of everything, in Yeshua's time, says that the only way to be free of the past is by sacrifice. If you've done something that appears in the lawbook's list of prohibited actions, you go to the one temple in the one city, and you pay the tariff for the action, also listed in the lawbook. You buy a pigeon, or a bullock, or a ram, from the special animal dealers operating in the temple forecourt, and then you take it to the priests, who kill it for you, and because you have penitently given up the cost of the sacrifice, your action dies along with the animal.

And thus you stand right again with God. But Yeshua says that the HPtFtU is universal and pervasive, staining our thoughts as well as our actions, far in excess of the lawbook's listing; and he doesn't seem to be talking about sacrifice. At least, not a sacrifice that we can make. He doesn't seem to think that any number of dead doves can remake our relationship with our own history. Instead – to the horror of the pious people he talks to – he thinks that he can. Don't you know that only *God* can forgive us? someone is saying to him one day, when, at that moment, a shaft of sunlight suddenly appears in the darkness of the house where he is sitting. It isn't a sign of divine favour. It's a hole in the roof. The entrepreneurially-minded relations of a paraplegic have decided to jump the queue to see Yeshua by breaking their way in from above. In a tumble of thatch and dust and plaster particles, down comes a whole mattress, on ropes. Yes, says Yeshua wearily, because taking away guilt would be even harder, wouldn't it, than taking away this gentleman's paralysis? But, just to make the point: get up, sir. Walk. And hey, take the bed with you, please.

And now, at last, he turns toward the one city. He and his friends make for the dry yellow town on the desert hill where the empire's governor keeps the uneasy peace with the authorities of the one temple. It's where this story was always going. It's where a *christos*, a *moshiakh*, would have to declare himself. It's where power is. It's where the religion of the God of everything has its focus. It is the place where actions stop being provisional, experimental, retrievable, and become definite, final. It's where this drama, whatever it is, must find its ending.

They arrive at the walls, but it's too late in the evening for the entrance Yeshua has in mind, so they wait till the next day in the straggly settlement outside the gates. Then in they go, Yeshua and the nucleus of twenty or so men and women who have been following him about. The narrow stone streets are packed with visitors who've come in from the province for the biggest festival of the year, a festival of death averted, in which the people of the one God remember how he saved them by smiting the rest; and the visitors see, well, something like a parade, with Yeshua riding on a borrowed donkey, and the friends around him shouting make way, make way. Who's this? It's another bloody prophet. It's that crazy preacher who says we don't need the law. It's the rabbi from up north who heals people. What, the river-dipping one? No, he's dead, this is another one. It's a king! Rubbish, kings ride on horses, not donkeys. But there are prophecies about donkeys. Maybe he's the one. Oh come on. This fellow? Where's his sword? It's the king, it's the king! Keep your voice down, idiot. Better get the children indoors, just in case.

Is it a king? The scene is hard to read. It's like a royal progress and a parody of a royal progress, all at once. Yeshua is doing exactly what a *christos* would do if he were making a momentum play, gambling on snowballing crowd support. Yet the details are off-script somehow, from the donkey, to the way that only some of the friends seem to be shouting the slogans you'd expect, to the way that the man himself doesn't have his face set in the shining megawatt mask of charisma. It isn't clear what's happening. But *something* is, and though only a portion of the crowd are young enough, or hopeful enough, or desperate enough, or unwary enough, to give Yeshua their acclaim, quite a lot of them are curious enough to follow and see what comes next: for the parade, or procession, or whatever it is, is clearly heading for the temple, up the twisting alleyways to the top of the city, and the narrow gateway where the press of yellow house walls and tile roofs opens out all at once into the wide forecourt of the one God's most sacred place. The two guards on duty let the mob through without a word – those kinds of numbers are their own permission – but they send a runner, quick, to the Chief Priest's office; and he, looking down from his window, sees a human flood pouring out suddenly from the entry point to fill the flagstones of the courtyard and jostle against the pens where the animals are kept. In the midst of the flood a man is getting off a donkey. The Chief Priest has seen bigger crowds, but this one is quite big enough to do some damage if things turn ugly. Uh-oh, he thinks, and sends a runner of his own to the governor.

Yeshua looks around. He sees the doves in their wicker cages, and the half-grown spring lambs in their straw, and the nervous cattle sidling, kept perpetually antsy by the smell of blood that drifts out of the temple's doors. He sees the money-change stalls where, before you can even buy your animal for the sacrifice, you have to swap the emperor's dirty coinage for the temple's own clean currency, good nowhere else. He sees the whole apparatus for keeping this one little walled acre of ground separate from the compromised, colonised world outside. And he begins to shout. Do you call this pure? Do you think any of this keeps you clean? Do you think any of this keeps *that* at bay? – waving his arms out at the city, the hills, the entire empire. Nothing is pure! This is the house of the loving father who welcomes home his lost children! This is the house of my father, and your father! Do you think you can *sell* his forgiveness? Do you think there is a *price* for peace with him? It cannot be bought! It cannot be sold! It can only be given! These are *thieves*! They promise you are buying what can only be given! God gives freely! Tear down the temple, and He will still give you all you need! And in a kind of frenzy, Yeshua starts yanking at the timbers of the nearest stall. The board serving as a counter gives way, and little piles of silver go spinning and clinking onto the paving slabs, followed by the dealer in a diving crouch. Here we go, thinks the Chief Priest, and he hopes that the squads of soldiers the governor will have sent to the nearby streets understand that they must not enter the temple to quell the riot.

But the crowd don't join in. Yeshua hasn't pressed their buttons. He's here at the heart of what matters to them, and if he'd said the right things, if he'd filled them with enough righteous wrath to overcome their fears, the city could have been his, at least until the governor brought up violence's trained professionals. But he didn't. He ranted inexplicably about a bit of the temple scene everyone knows has to be there, and he said something threatening about the precious building. They don't join in. They don't want to join in. They just look at him; and then, muttering, they start to drain back out of the yard. Yeshua has not sparked the uprising. All he has done is to mark himself out in authority's eyes as a menace. The Chief Priest would have him arrested now, if he could, but Yeshua's friends are escorting him away in the retreating crowd, and it wouldn't do to inflame things just when they're dying down nicely. Finding him again in the warren of yellow alleys will be a problem – but an hour later the Chief Priest has a piece of luck, when one of the friends comes back with a tip-off about where they're planning to be that night. He isn't what I thought, the man says, furious and betrayed.

The evening sees Yeshua and the friends celebrating the festival in a borrowed upstairs room. His mood is strange, and they keep looking at him, perturbed, as they eat the roast lamb and yeastless bread with bitter herbs, and they share the cup of wine, and tell the story of how the one God long ago brought His people out of captivity. He doesn't seem like a person whose plans have failed; he is not confused or despondent at all. Yet he is full of trembling intensity. Everything he says seems deliberate and effortful, as if this dinner-

in-lieu-of-a-revolution were a part of something terrifying he was making himself do, step by step, word
by word, action by action. After supper he does
something that isn't in the festival ritual. He picks up
one of the flat loaves they haven't touched yet. This is
my body, he says, and he snaps it in half, using both
hands. He asks for the winecup. This is my blood, he
says. Do this when you remember me. It's one of those
likeness things again – but the friends don't think too
hard about what he means, because they're bursting
out with anxiety at the finality of the way he's talking.
Remember you? *Remember* you? Where are you going?
We won't leave you. Don't worry about today; it doesn't
matter. We won't leave you, teacher.

But they do. A few hours later, in the dark, on the
open ground at the edge of the city where they're
camped out, a patrol of temple guards find them – and
the friends, looking to Yeshua for guidance and getting
none, hesitate, waver, and run for it, leaving him alone
in custody.

For the rest of that night he gets frogmarched from
place to place: to a quick convocation of the temple's
lawcourt at the Chief Priest's house, and then onwards
to an equally quick interview with the yawning governor, called from his bed to confirm that the empire's
civil arm agrees with the temple's judgement. This
haste not indicating that Yeshua's is a particularly urgent or important case, but, precisely, that the city's two
authorities want to keep it minimised, with this minor
northern rabbi who's made a nuisance of himself

briskly disposed of before daylight comes. He isn't especially maltreated; he isn't singled out for particular cruelties. The ordinarily bad things that happen to prisoners happen to him, that's all. He gets punched a few times to keep him moving, and worked over a bit to encourage contrition and co-operation before his conversations with power. Maybe he loses some skin, some teeth, has his nose broken, gets a few cracked ribs. But it's routine, it's perfunctory, it isn't the inventive horrors of a torturer really going to town. It's just a consequence of his new position as an object, a still-living being which is already pretty much a thing as power acts on it. This body is already beyond human consideration; it need not be treated gently, or with an eye to its future survival, because it has no future. The whole process is marking it out quite clearly for death, and so it does not matter what happens to it. The only oddity is that Yeshua, who talked so eloquently, who shadow-boxed with words so deftly on occasion, refuses entirely to defend himself. All night long he only echoes back the accusations. You threatened the temple. You say so, says Yeshua. You're a blasphemer, a Sabbath-breaker, an enemy of the law. You say so. You think you can forgive sins. You say so. You claim to be king. You say so. You are a menace to public order. You say so. All night long, a human mirror-wall, reflecting back what's in front of it, except that all the while he inclines his bruised head and concentrates on whoever is speaking as if they were the only person in the world. He does not need to ask what they want him to do for them, now, since they are telling him the answer, all the time. We need you to be guilty. We need you to be the mess that must be removed so that the world can work smoothly. We need you to be the unclean shadow of our righteousness, our good imperial order. We need you to be dirt, disease, crime, shame, humiliation, chaos, darkness, so that we can be virtue, certainty, light. We need you to be *in* the dirt, soon. It's nothing personal.

Daylight finds him in a procession again, but this time no one could mistake him for a king. He's stumbling along under the weight of his own instrument of execution, a great big wooden thing he can hardly lift, with an escort of the empire's soldiers, and the bystanders who've come blinking out of the lodgings where they spent the festival night don't see their hopes, or even the possibility of their hopes, parading by. They see their disappointment, they see their frustration. They see everything in themselves that is too weak or too afraid to confront the strapping paratroopers; and much though they hate the soldiers, they hate him more, for his pathetic slide into victimhood. Word of his loose living, his impiety, his pleasure in bad company goes round in whispers. And just look at him. There's something disgusting about him, don't you think? Something that makes you squirm inside. Something . . . furtive. He's so pale and sickly-looking, with that dried blood round his mouth. He looks like a paedophile being led away by the police. He looks like something from under a rock; as if he doesn't deserve the daylight. He's a blot on the new day. Someone kicks

his arse as he goes by, and whoops, down he goes, flat
on his nose with the cross pinning him like a struggling
insect, and let's face it, it's funny. Yeshua is a joke. He's
less a messiah, more a patch of something nasty on the
pavement. And as he struggles on he recognises every
roaring, jeering face. He knows our names. He knows
our histories.

And since, as well as being a weak and frightened
man, he's also the love that makes the world, to whom
all times and places are equally present, he isn't just
feeling the anger and spite and unbearable self-disgust
of this one crowd on this one Friday morning in
Palestine; he's turning his bruised face toward the
whole human crowd, past and present and to come,
and accepting everything we have to throw at him,
everything we fear we deserve ourselves. The doors
of his heart are wedged open wide, and in rushes
the whole pestilential flood, the vile and roiling tide
of cruelties and failures and secrets. Let me take that
from you, he is saying. Give that to me instead. Let me
carry it. Let me be to blame instead. I am big enough.
I am wide enough. I am not what you were told. I
am not your king or your judge. I am the father who
longs for every last one of his children. I am the friend
who will never leave you. I am the light behind the
darkness. I am the shining your shame cannot extin-
guish. I am the ghost of love in the torture chamber. I
am change and hope. I am the refining fire. I am the
door where you thought there was only wall. I am what
comes after deserving. I am the earth that drinks up

the bloodstain. I am gift without cost. I am. I am. I am. Before the foundations of the world, I am.

But it is killing him all the same. He never promised that you would be safe, if you tried to live without fear. The soldiers lead him out of the city gate, and, laboriously, slipping and sliding, with crunching blows from spear butts to motivate him, they drive him up the small cone of Skull Hill, where death sentences are carried out. They tie him onto the cross and plant it upright. It's the empire's punishment for rebellious slaves, slow and nasty by design, devised to be a spectacle of days-long struggle and gasping to passers-by. On a cross you choke to death, when you're finally too tired to heave your own weight up to take the next breath. Yeshua's cross has a sign on it, over his head. HERE'S YOUR KING, it says, in all the languages of the province. The Chief Priest didn't want it, but the governor has a point to make. And Yeshua hangs there. He twists against the ropes to snatch the precious air, which whistles in his flattened nose.

He cannot do anything deliberate now. The strain of his whole weight on his outstretched arms hurts too much. The pain fills him up, displaces thought, as much for him as it has for everyone else who has ever been stuck to one of these horrible contrivances, or for anyone else who dies in pain from any of the world's grim arsenal of possibilities. And yet he goes on taking in. It is not what he does, it is what he is. He is all open door: to sorrow, suffering, guilt, despair, horror, everything that cannot be escaped, and he does not even try to escape it, he turns to meet it, and claims it all as his own. This is mine now, he is saying; and he embraces it with all that is left in him, each dark act, each dripping memory, as if it were something precious, as if it were itself the loved child tottering homeward on the road. But there is so much of it. So many injured children; so many locked rooms; so much lonely anger; so many bombs in public places; so much vicious zeal; so many bored teenagers at roadblocks; so many drunk girls at parties someone thought they could have a little fun with; so many jokes that go too far; so much ruining greed; so much sick ingenuity; so much burned skin. The world he claims, claims him. It burns and stings, it splinters and gouges, it locks him round and drags him down.

Because this is not a rich man's offer of something he can easily spare. This is not some supernatural personage being temporarily inconvenienced. This is love going where we go, all of us, when we end. Yeshua is long past trying to show what lies beyond the limits of the world. He is travelling into limit himself, now, deeper and deeper, and the limits are tightening in on him, tightening down to a ribcage that won't fill, tightening on him as consequences tighten on anyone. He's gone to the place our sorrows lead to at their worst: guilt's dead-end, panic's no-exit loop, despair's junkyard where everything is busted. There's nothing to keep him company there but the light he's always felt shining beneath things. But the light is going. He's so deep down now in the geology of woe, so buried beneath the mountains' weight of it, that the pressure is squeezing out his feeling for the light. There's nothing left of it for him but a speck, a pinpoint the world grinds in on itself, a dot dimming as the strata of the dark are piled heavier and heavier on it. And then it goes out. Of course it does. Love can't repair death. Death is stronger than love. We all know that. But Yeshua didn't, until now. This is the first time in his entire life he's ever felt alone. Now there is no love song. There is no kind father. There is just a man on a cross, dying in pain; a foolish man who chose to give up life and breath to be a carcass on a pole. The yellow walls of the city blur with Yeshua's tears, and he opens his mouth and howls the news – new only to him – that we are abandoned in a dark place where help never comes.

The friends creep out at dusk and ask for the body, promising anonymous burial and no fuss. They're allowed to carry it away, wrapped in a tube of linen that slowly stains from inside. Skull Hill sees lots of such corteges. There's only time to stick what's left of Yeshua hastily in a rock tomb by the highway. Washing the corpse properly and laying it out will have to wait; the holy Saturday is coming, and no one wants any confrontations.

All day long, the next day, the city is quiet. The air above the city lacks the usual thousand little trails of smoke from cookfires. Hymns rise from the temple. Families are indoors. The soldiers are back in barracks. The Chief Priest grows hoarse with singing. The governor plays chess with his secretary and dictates letters.

The free bread the temple distributed to the poor has gone stale by midday, but tastes all right dipped in water or broth. Death has interrupted life only as much as it ever does. We die one at a time and disappear, but the life of the living continues. The earth turns. The sun makes its way towards the western horizon no slower or faster than it usually does.

Early Sunday morning, one of the friends comes back with rags and a jug of water and a box of the grave spices that are supposed to cut down on the smell. She's braced for the task. But when she comes to the grave she finds that the linen's been thrown into the corner and the body is gone. Evidently anonymous burial isn't quite anonymous enough, after all. She sits outside in the sun. The insects have woken up, here at the edge of the desert, and a bee is nosing about in a lily like silk thinly tucked over itself, but much more perishable. It won't last long. She takes no notice of the feet that appear at the edge of her vision. That's enough now, she thinks. That's more than enough.

Don't be afraid, says Yeshua. Far more can be mended than you know.

She is weeping. The executee helps her to stand up.

6

Et Cetera

I have cheated, of course. I have simplified and selected and heightened the story, in the telling of it, to make the emotional outline of it as clear as I can. I have rephrased and rewritten, I have anachronised and estranged, to try to peel away the lingering familiarity which might prevent you from hearing it fresh. Above all I have narrated the story's meaning rather than its naked events; I have folded the meaning Christians give it *into* the events, rather than leaving it up to you to decide how to interpret them.

But this is true to the nature of the story as you'll find it in the New Testament's four biographies of Yeshua/Jesus. For the first thing that needs to be observed about the story is that it is not in any obvious way an interpretation bolted on top of a plain account by witnesses of things simply happening. In particular, it is not a fanciful later claim that its protagonist is God incarnate layered over a previous story in which he was just a good man. The God/man mixture in the story is very strange, and people have been wanting to separate the elements back out again and to make its central figure more straightforward and homogenous for a long, long time. For pretty much the whole length of Christian history, in fact, from the Gnostics of the second century AD declaring him to be all divine and

Arians in the fourth century declaring him all human, to Islam in the seventh century insisting that he was just a prophet, right through to the deists of the eighteenth century and the Unitarians of the nineteenth century hailing him as a 'great moral teacher', and Philip Pullman five minutes ago carefully dismantling him into twins in *The Good Man Jesus and the Scoundrel Christ*. (With neither half divine, but all the dodgy and sinister organised-religion stuff concentrated in 'Christ', leaving 'Jesus' free to embody the let's-be-nice-to-each-other aspect of him that, you know, you kind of can't help respecting. Pullman's Jesus ends up as an atheist. He's a *really* good man.)

In the air now, there's a general feeling that somebody or other in the early church, probably St Paul, retrospectively glued Godhood onto poor Jesus, appropriating what was clearly a perfectly ordinary and unmysterious career as a Jewish preacher, and using it as a vehicle for weird shit. Jesus goes about encouraging people to be kind and forgiving; then, when he's safely dead, he gets signed up as the lead of an unlikely cosmic drama he'd have been horrified by if he'd ever known about it. Lift the lid of the interpretation, and there's the man underneath, a minor first-century religious reformer with a bit of a bee in his bonnet about gentleness. A well-intentioned and irrelevant person from the pre-Enlightenment ages of superstition. Result: happiness.

The trouble is that the historical sequence by which we get the story is exactly the other way round. The interpretation came first, before the narratives about him

150

wandering around preachin' and teachin'. Of all the documents in the New Testament, the oldest are St Paul's letters ('Epistles') to the various early churches. They were written in the fifties AD, fifteen to twenty years after the crucifixion, and they are metaphor-heavy discourses about what Jesus was and what he meant. They don't have the whole elaborated theological vocabulary for describing him that came later – partly because they themselves are helping invent that vocabulary – and they certainly don't have the neat three-cornered diagram of the 'Holy Trinity' that Christianity is going to end up with, with God's making, mending and sustaining aspects tidied up into 'Father', 'Son' and 'Holy Spirit'. But they, the letters, do have an absolutely definite set of convictions about him that they are casting around for adequate words to express. That Jesus's actions in the world were God's own actions in the world; that where Jesus was present, God was directly present too; that his death and return from death were an initiative by God to take from humanity the weight of guilt and shame and disgust, and to show us a life larger than law. This cluster of propositions is Christianity's first layer of organised words and understandings. It, not the biographies, is the foundation. Which means that the strange God/man mixture is there *in* the foundation. It may not be true, it may still be a piece of after-the-event fabrication or misunderstanding, but it is not an addition to the story. It is, itself, the thing the story is struggling to report.

We have the biographies ('Gospels') because early

Christians – i.e. early believers in the God/man mixture in Jesus – wanted to illustrate it in story, to bring home (as only story can for human beings) its emotional force. They had some kind of a collection of his sayings, in the fifties and sixties of the first century, which they probably passed around in many slightly different copies. Now they expanded it, in coarse and workaday Greek, into a continuous narrative. This happened four times over, starting in the seventies with the one the New Testament calls the Gospel of Mark, and ending with John late in the nineties or early in the 100s, each unfolding of the story making a slightly different selection from the bag of memories and traditions, each tending to emphasise a particular theme in its portrait of him, each doing some topical work in the disputes of the decade it was written in. Note the language: the trade tongue of the whole eastern end of the Roman empire, not the Semitic dialect Yeshua actually spoke. The story already had its travelling clothes on. This is where Yeshua becomes Jesus. Note the timing too. In the late sixties, the long-awaited explosion had finally come in Palestine, with the outbreak of the first of three full-scale revolts, each of which would be suppressed with extreme prejudice by several legions of violence's trained professionals.* When the Gospel stories started to be written, Jeru-

---

* In the last of the three, the Bar Kokhba uprising of AD 132–6, an actual old-school military *moshiakh* appeared. The death toll was around six hundred thousand.

salem was already a ruin and the temple was rubble; the province's countryside was beginning to be ethnically cleansed. The landscape of small towns and small-town synagogues, populated by yearning, fearful, angry people, was ceasing to exist. The Gospel writers were recreating a lost place and time when they described Jesus's journeys fifty, sixty, seventy years earlier. The interpretation was always fused with the events.

Moreover, even if you try to discard everything in the biographies which is explicitly devoted to storytelling Jesus's divinity, and just concentrate on the bits which must have come most uncontentiously from the lost sayings-collection, you *still* don't get back to a layer in which he's just a wise person dispensing wisdom. The striking thing about the advice on behaviour he gives is how catastrophically impractical most of it is as a guide to the good life, if by a good life you mean something reasonably self-protecting, and concerned with next year, and with living in some kind of viable community. 'Great moral teachers' tend to be concerned with respecting your parents (Confucius), defining duty and justice (Socrates), detaching yourself from desire (the Buddha), discovering law (Moses), and getting people to see themselves as accountable individuals rather than fractions of a tribe (Muhammad). 'If someone asks for your coat, give them your shirt too' is *not* 'great moral teaching' in this sense. It is either foolishness, or something else.

Needless to say, the something else might be just: a

mistake. C. S. Lewis produced one of the great Bad Arguments of all time when he proposed that Jesus must either have been (a) exactly what he said he was – what he said he was being, perhaps, slightly neatened up for the occasion – or (b) the wickedest person who ever lived. A pause for thought lasting no more than a millisecond produces, slap bang in the excluded middle that Lewis was trying to rule out, but which wobbles and gurgles all the same like the vast wide-open distended logical midriff that it is, an immediate option (c). That is, that Jesus really thought his burning, urgent, lover's perception of humanity belonged in some way to the God of everything, but was just plain *wrong*. You can imagine any number of ways in which, in a charged and desperate and theologically expectant environment, an intense young man might persuade himself that it was up to him to reconcile God and humanity. Making him not the messiah, but just a very silly boy. Or indeed – option (d) – the mistake may after all have been the early church's, and a Judaic Jesus with something completely different on his mind may simply have been lost in the translation from memory to words. But the story they told, once they told a story at all, was committedly the story of God-among-us, God entering into our lives and deaths.

Hold on, though. Aren't there a zillion other 'Gospels', arbitrarily ignored and suppressed and edited out of the picture to produce the illusion of theological orthodoxy? You know, heaving with secret lore and hot sex? Well . . . no. Not really. Sorry. The publishers who've tried to cash in on the post-*Da Vinci Code* interest in Early Christian Freakiness by bringing out mass-market editions of *The Gospel of Thomas*, *The Gospel of Judas*, *The Gospel of Mary Magdalene* and so on have had to work really hard to make the stuff seem thrilling. For one thing, hardly any of these books actually tell a consecutive but alternative version of Jesus's life story. They don't draw on different facts, details and memories about him; they were mostly written much later, in the late 100s, the 200s, even the 300s, and they are called 'gospels' because 'gospel' had by then become the name of something prestigious and authoritative, in rather the way that, *On the Origin of Species* being an extremely famous and influential book, we have – a quick Googling reveals – a slew of books called things like *The Origin of Wealth*, *The Origins of Political Order*, *The Origins of the World's Mythologies*, *The Origins of the British* and *The Origins of the First World War*. What these other 'gospels' are instead is a series of pamphlets in which Jesus serves as the mouthpiece for the authors' preoccupations, usually magical or esoteric. It isn't that they cast an intriguingly different light on someone who is recognisably the same person as the one in the New Testament. They are worlds away in mood and tone and attitude.

The Jesus of the orthodox story treats people with deep attention even when angry. Their Jesus zaps people with his divine superpowers if they irritate him. Orthodox Jesus says that everyone needs the love of God, and God loves everyone. Their Jesus has an inner circle you can be admitted to if you collect enough crisp packets. Orthodox Jesus likes wine, parties, and grilled fish for breakfast. Their Jesus thinks that human flesh and its appetites are icky. Orthodox Jesus is disconcertingly unbothered about sexuality, and conducts his own sexual life, if he has one, off the page. Their Jesus can generate women to have sex with *out of his own ribs*, in a way that suggests the author had trouble talking to girls. Orthodox Jesus says, 'Don't be afraid. I am always with you.' The Jesus of these documents says, 'Advance, Blue Adept, to the 17th Jade Portal of Amazingness, and give the secret signal with your thumbs.'* Read much of the rival 'gospels', and you start to think that the Church Fathers who decided what went into the New Testament had one of the easiest editorial jobs on record. It wasn't a question of suppression or exclusion, so much as of seeing what did and didn't belong inside the bounds of a basically coherent story.

But a strange story. Still, it cannot be denied, a very strange story; with a peculiar and untidy vision of the nature of God at the centre of it. Claiming that a provincial rabbi somehow embodies the impulse behind billions of years of history and unthinkable expanses of space does not have much philosophical dignity to it as a position. It is – let's be honest – the kind of silly thing that a cult would assert. It entails a very odd, even

---

* In effect. Believe me, I have done you a favour by condensing a vast amount of Gnostic wibble into this convenient joke.

comical, blending of the universal and the extremely local. It deliberately entangles unlikenesses. To have a creator who becomes a creature mixes up the conceptual layers of ordinary reality. It pokes a hole in reality and pulls some of the background through to form a lovely rosette; it ties a Möbius-knot in the fabric, like the paradox Bertrand Russell came unstuck on, when he was trying to compile a complete axiomatic basis for logic using set theory, and ran into the problem of the set that has itself for one of its members.* Or you could put the paradox in literary terms, and say that this is a story which has its author as one of the characters – not parachuted in all post-modernistically, to twist and trick and tease and hint that the whole structure is airy nothing, but the opposite, with the author brain-hurtingly embedded on exactly the same terms as the other characters, his presence having the effect of making the story *more* real, *more* consequential.

What's more, the mixture involved has the psychological power that matter-out-of-place famously does. It can be perceived as contaminating precious things that are supposed to be kept apart from each other. Things that are kept apart or set apart are 'holy' – that's what the word 'holy' means – and the Christian move of giving God a human body literally messes with holiness, at least as the other two monotheisms define it. For two thousand years, the Christian story

---

* A problem which has a lot more bearing on Christian belief than the sodding teapot, by the way.

is going to strike first Jews and then Muslims too as a besmirching of the purity and absoluteness of the one God with cheap, nasty stuff from the pagan playbook, where gods walk the earth bamboozling kings and jumping on maidens. You can see their point. They had only just finished laboriously picking the human bad behaviour out of their picture of the God of everything, and along came Christians, putting human, fleshy qualities back in. How *can* God beget a son, asks the Qur'an? And it isn't just quibbling over the powers of divinity. It's saying that God stands (and must stand, if He's to be truly God) apart from, and distinct from, the whole category of biological existence. Christians disagree. We disagree because the God/man mixture in Jesus brings us something more precious than conceptual purity: hope in trouble, consolation in suffering, help in anguish. It brings us a way out of the far worse and more destructive paradoxes of theodicy. But it does lay our story alongside some disconcertingly similar stories out of mythology, and it requires us to ask ourselves, clearly and carefully, what kind of story we think ours is.

As freethinkers have been gleefully reminding everyone for the last two centuries – always, somehow, with the air of playing a killer card no one has ever noticed before – the New Testament's story of Jesus is not, to put it mildly, the only one humanity has ever come up with about a dying god. The ancient Greeks had Adonis bleeding out onto the springtime earth, and coming back to life three days later having renewed the world. The Egyptians had Osiris, ripped into shreds and scattered like holy flesh-confetti into all the nooks and crannies of matter. The Vikings had Odin getting wisdom by hanging nailed to a tree. It's a common mythological move, a cultural basic, an anthropological golden oldie. Transcendent power goes down into the dark and allows itself to be extinguished, but then returns all the stronger, having incorporated into itself the strength of the opposing principle. A frequent Christian response, when this is pointed out, is to argue that all the *other* stories are foreshadowings or echoes of ours, which happens to be the one true story. But this, to me, seems rather obviously to set the big red Special Pleading alarm flashing, and to sound the klaxon of bullshit. I think a better answer is just to agree that universal is universal is universal. Everybody dies; everybody tells stories about gods; everybody is going to try, at some point, to make story-sense of death by subjecting one of the lustrous figures of the gods to it. The usual point of gods is that they're immortal, which will make the death of one of them bring out all the more fiercely the existential scandal which is our own death. Gods, in anthropological terms, are where we put in concentrated form our sense of what our own being, our own aliveness, is. A god dies: being encounters non-being. Everyone sits up in their seats and leans forward, because the drama is our own. So perhaps that's what Christianity is, the traditional god-dies theme being installed for the God of everything? If so, then the story I've just told *is* a myth. We can categorise Jesus's adventures as forming an imaginative pattern like the pattern of the story of Odin, one whose function is to embody a deep piece of human meaning-discovery. One which is true (or maybe 'true') so far as it embodies true perception, rather than because it corresponds to any actual event.

But though Jesus's story certainly has some mythic parallels, and acquired some mythic resonances as it became a whole culture's founding artefact, it does not read like a myth. It's the wrong shape, in a number of different ways. For a start, it doesn't happen in the special time set aside for myths, the dream-time, the long-ago zone off to the side of calendar history where gods and heroes strutted their stuff. What year was it when Odin hung on the tree? The question does not compute. It's a category error, like asking what colour accountancy is. Jesus's story, by contrast, happens at a definite historical address. As *Monty Python's Life of Brian* puts it, 'Judea, AD 33, teatime'. From our point of view twenty centuries later, this may seem fairly misty and far-off, but it's firmly within the documented, busy, event-stuffed course of human history, the zone of prose and politics, in which people like ourselves worked and worried as we do. Part of the point of the story is that it happens in ordinary time, amidst people who are already precoccupied and are not expecting anything special to come along. The story is about God coming into what's ordinary, and changing it.

This same ordering of things – extraordinary into

ordinary – applies, in fact, to Jesus as a protagonist, and makes him very different from a myth's hero. In myth, our ordinary preoccupations get projected outwards in extraordinary form. They're amplified into fantasy. Here, what is emphatically not our view of the world, not our set of natural priorities, *not us*, breaks inward into the world of our ordinary experience, and dwells among us, 'full of grace and truth'. Instead of surging about looking superlative, as mythic heroes are prone to do, flexing enormous muscles or giving smiles of groin-melting beauty, Jesus does his best to complicate and perturb any worshipful reactions he might get, by asking awkward questions. 'Why do you call me good?' 'Who do you say that I am?' It may be normal for us as human beings to be worshipful, deferring to those in our local troupe of primates we perceive as being grander, stronger, wiser, braver, more glamorous than us; but Jesus, who in the Christian view is the one person who fully deserves worship, goes out of his way to demonstrate that he does not need it. We're back at the non-rivalrous majesty of the creator. Jesus is not in the business of competing for our admiration, or for anything else. Nothing he has or is, in the story, is extracted from other people's reactions to him. He shows us a vision of the good which does not ask us to bow down – though we may want to – but, over and over again, to stand up. (And to take the bed with us.)

If it isn't a myth, then perhaps it is a tragedy. On the immediate face of it, this seems an unlikely category to find it in. Hello? It has a happy ending? Yes it does; it has the original 'eucatastrophe', or unexpected turning of events to the good. But it doesn't have its happy end instead of the grim outcome that leaves the stage piled with bodies in a tragedy. It doesn't procure its happy end by saying that with one bound Jesus was free, or that his friends rode up with a fast horse and a step-ladder; or that, in any way, the necessities tragedy pays attention to, the necessities of pride and fear and anger and distrust, were prevented from having their full dire effect, and unrolling their consequences to their last inevitable gasp. The happy end of Jesus's story is not a daydream of escape. It's not like the bowdlerised eighteenth-century version of *King Lear* where Cordelia's husband turns up to save her in the nick of time, and Lear goes contentedly off with her to live at her house. Yeshua's story has its happy ending *because of* its tragic one: happiness after tragedy, on top of it, through it, achievable only by going to the very end of the tragic road.

Like a tragedy, it stirs up pity and terror in us. Like a tragedy it requires us to contemplate the world's darkness. Like a tragedy, it draws attention to *waste*. It shows us a life that need not have been extinguished being extinguished, without particular malice, by the normal processes of the world. It shows us that accident, injustice, spoilage, are all standard, all in the pitiably usual course of things. Here it's important that Jesus's death was an obscure one, when it happened. He's not an Oedipus or a Prince Hamlet, someone falling from greatness. His death belongs beside the early cutting-short of the millions of lives of people too poor or too unimportant ever to have been recorded in the misleading story we call history; people only mourned by others as brief as themselves, and therefore gone from human memory as if they had never been. Jesus dies like a migrant worker who suffocates in a freight container, like a garbage-picker caught in a slide, like a child with an infected finger, like a beggar the bus reverses over. Or, of course, like all the other slaves ever punished by crucifixion, a fate so *low*, said Cicero, that no well-bred person should ever even mention it. Christians believe that Jesus's death is, among other things, a way for God to mention it, loudly and with no good breeding at all, a declaration by the maker of the world, in pain and solidarity, that to Him the measure of the waste of history is not the occasional tragedies of kings but the routine losses of every day. It is not an accident that Christianity began as a religion 'for slaves and women'.* It is not an accident that, wherever it travels, it appeals first to untouchables. The last shall be first and the first shall be last, said Jesus. You'd have to turn the world upside down to do justice to God's sense of the tragedy of it.

And when the story does turn the world upside down, or the order of nature anyway, by telling us that Jesus lives again, it isn't suggesting that he didn't really die, or that we won't really die. The happy end-

---

* Nietzsche. He thinks this is a criticism. It's a compliment.

ing makes a promise sized to the utmost extent of our darkest convictions. It says 'Yes, *and . . .*' to tragedy. It promises, bizarrely enough, that love is stronger than death. But it does not promise that death is imaginary, that death is avoidable, that death is temporary. To have death, this once, be reversed is to let us feel the depth of our ordinary loss in it, not to pretend it away. Some people ask nowadays what kind of a religion it is that chooses an instrument of torture for its symbol, as if the cross on churches must represent some kind of endorsement. The answer is: one that takes the existence of suffering seriously.

And this is why I feel comfortably orthodox in choosing to tell the story without any of the emphasis you may have been expecting on promises of eternal life. Like all good stories, it can't just be understood one way. It creates a repertoire of possible understandings, and right from the beginning these understandings have ranged across several things Jesus could have meant when he said he came to bring 'life in abundance', life without limits. There are many ways life can be limited, and only one of them has to do with duration. You can take the story as meaning that if you believe in Jesus you'll live for ever with him in heaven. Many Christians have and many Christians do. You can; but you don't have to. You can also believe that Jesus's death and resurrection 'redeem'* us right now,

---

* A word meaning 'to buy out of slavery'. But putting issues of etymology aside, this is the last footnote of the chapter, and therefore

in our lives, by acting to free us from our pasts; from
the weight, the confinement, the limits, of the HPtFtU.
And this too is orthodoxy, this too is part of the ordinary core of the religion rather than its avant-garde
fringe. It's what makes sense to me. I'm a very this-
worldly Christian. I am averagely afraid of dying, but
I don't believe because I expect, or want, to have an
unlimited future, tweedling about with a harp while
the stars of the Western Spiral Arm burn out one by
one. I believe because I know I've got a past and a

---

the last chance to address the question some of you may feel should
have been its main attraction. Viz., is the damn story *true*? Not what
its history is, or what literary category it belongs in; whether it
actually happened. Well, I don't know. I think it did, miracles, resurrection and all. But I don't know. And you will have to judge
for yourself, too, because although Christianity makes a historical claim, and therefore in principle is falsifiable in the way that a
purely philosophical belief in God's existence isn't, in practice it's
highly unlikely that an archaeological discovery or a lost document
is going to come along and cause the religion to implode suddenly.
That's Dan Brown territory. One move, please note, is not available
to you – at least you can't make it and expect it to be decisive. You
can't just say, this story contains physical impossibilities (miracles,
resurrection from the dead) and thus *a priori* must be counted
among the impossible things a rational person shouldn't believe before breakfast. That is to assume the untruth of the story's own
contention that there is a maker of nature who, this once, was able
to alter nature's normal operations. In other words, the argument
from impossibility depends on a faith position adopted before-
hand, which rather reduces its logical grip on the world. So despite
it being a historical question we're trying to settle here rather than
a philosophical one, we're back on undecidable ground. You can
base your judgement on your sense of *probabilities*, certainly. Induc-
tion holds even if deduction doesn't. But also, maybe, you should
judge whether you feel the story tells you anything urgent or important.

present in which the HPtFtU did and does its usual work, and I want a way of living which opens out more widely and honestly and lovingly than I can manage for myself, which widens rather than narrowing with each destructive decision. Like the Christian Aid slogan says, I believe in life *before* death. For me and for everyone else. I don't care about heaven. I want, I need, the promise of mending.

Mended is not the same thing as never broken. We are not being promised that it will be as if the bad stuff never happened. It's amnesty that's being offered, not amnesia; hope, not pretence. The story of your life will still be the story of your life, permanently. It will still have the kinks and twists and corners you gave it. The consequences of your actions, for you and for other people, will roll inexorably on. God can't take these away, or your life would not be your life, you would not be you, the world would not be the world. He can only take from us – take over for us – the guilt and the fear, so that we can start again free, in hope. So that we are freed to try again and fail again, better. He can only overwhelm the HPtFtU with grace.

Which we can now define. Grace is forgiveness we can't earn. Grace is the weeping father on the road. Grace is tragedy accepted with open arms, and somehow turned to good. Grace is what the wasteful death on Skull Hill did.

7

The International League of the Guilty, Part Two

A message of universal forgiveness? What could possibly go wrong?

A version of Christian history assembles itself very readily these days which jumps off from famous Christian-committed iniquities of the present, like clerical child abuse, and works backward in time finding counterpart outrages all the way to the point, two thousand years ago, when the memory of Jesus was first organised into the thing called 'the church'. Outrages and miseries; and nothing significant *but* outrages and miseries. This version of the Christian centuries is filled exclusively with conquistadors and crusaders, inquisitors and witch-finders, with bigotry and burnings and fear preached from the pulpit, with libraries on fire and science suppressed, with vicious battle between armies supposedly committed to brotherly love. If you believe that this record of hate is the whole truth about what happens when Christianity exists as an organised presence in human society, then it is going to be very hard to see why anyone would sign up to it with reasonably good intentions. And it's going to be just about inexplicable that, given all the bad stuff, Christians nevertheless believe that our church is something precious. Unless, of course, we secretly approve of the bad stuff.

Unless in our heart of hearts we're actually in favour of massacre and prejudice and exclusion.

Well, we aren't; or, more accurately, we aren't *specially*. We're only as darkly susceptible to that stuff as everyone else is. But here I both do and don't want to argue with the current caricature of Christian history. It's only untrue in being partial. I could certainly insist on the reality of the good stuff in the religion's record, which is often harder to see, having succeeded and thus faded indistinguishably into the background of our common sense. I could talk, for instance, about the invention of kindness as an ideal of behaviour to rival honour or dominance or stoicism. It may seem obvious to you now that you should be decent and polite to people you can get no use out of, but it wasn't always. Or I could bring up the way that the emphasis on people being loveable to God irrespective of what they deserve laid the groundwork for the idea of there being rights owed to people irrespective of their status, their behaviour, their capabilities. Or I could point to the slow, fitful, never wholehearted Christian campaign against slavery, which gradually, with massive backsliding and vast swathes of avoidable misery, expanded the prohibition on people owning people until now it is just about complete.[*] These are things to be proud of. But the bad stuff was, and is, real too. And

---

[*] The starting-point was a prohibition on Christians owning other Christians, which by 1400 or thereabouts made Europe the only continent without significant slave labour – just in time for

deep down it doesn't really help to draw attention to the existence of a credit side as well as a debit side in the moral ledger of the religion. If Christianity is anything, it's a refusal to see human behaviour as ruled by the balance sheet. We're not supposed to see the things we do as adding up into piles of good and evil we can subtract from each according to some kind of calculus to tell us how, on balance, we're doing. Experience is not convertible. Cruelty cannot be cancelled by equal and opposite amounts of being nice. The weight of sorrow is not lightened by happiness elsewhere. The bad stuff cannot be averaged. It can only be confessed.

On one level it is utterly unsurprising that Christian history is shot through with miseries, like a bloodstained roll of fabric. Christian history is, because all history is. It's the HPtFtU at work. Of course it's the HPtFtU. Christianity can shape human behaviour; it

---

the discovery of the New World, and the massive profits to be made from slavery there, to tempt European Christians into becoming owners of Africans on the grand scale, and for the whole institution to have to be laboriously extirpated all over again over the next five centuries. Yes, I really do get that it was Christians who committed the crime of the Atlantic trade, and for centuries found theological justifications for it. Yes, I really do see that the idea of a partial ban on owning *some* people is exclusive, vile and inadequate. But that was the circle that eventually widened till the ban became universal; and it was within Christian theology that the reasons for widening the circle were found. Only the Christian world was wicked enough to practise slavery in its bulk, industrialised, plantation-labour form, but once Christians decided against it, it was largely in imitation that the rest of the world started to reject it in its domestic, small-scale form. Slavery was abolished in Saudi Arabia, for example, in 1962.

can influence it, put a new frame around it, sometimes temper or channel or redirect it. It has the power that culture has, that imagination has, which is not a negligible power, for what people are is sculptable as well as scripted, we're creatures of chance and circumstance (and grace) as well as of our biology. But it can't abolish human behaviour. It can't eliminate human destructiveness. Accordingly, it hasn't. The first and most decisive feature of Christian history is that it has been composed at every stage of the actions of people. And people are subject to the HPtFtU. We don't stop being subject to it when we're Christians. People lie, cheat, extort, tyrannise, torture and kill. Christian people also lie, cheat, extort, tyrannise, torture and kill. People, given an institution to play with, turn it into a pecking order, a tool for personal power, an arena for politicking, an opportunity for spite, a capturable reservoir of rent and loot. So do Christian people. People fight wars. So do Christian people. People fight them for profit and territory, for the sake of abstract ideas, because they hate their neighbours; and so do Christian people.

When I see one of those passionate denunciations of religion which treats Christianity as the great gratuitous cause of all our sorrows, I mainly think: read more history, mate. Look at the vast record of conflict generated in every society that ever signed up for the opportunities and the costs of being more organised than hunter-gatherers. The logic of the complaint seems to be that because Christians believe in unreal things, the bad stuff Christians are involved in is unnecessary, and would stop if the unreal beliefs were taken away. Without pernicious Christianity we'd all be grouped round the white piano with John and Yoko. Yeah, right. The patterns of human bad behaviour are far wider and more ancient. I won't, myself, be convinced that the bloody wars Christians have fought over points of theology are uniquely the fault of the religion rather than of the species in general, unless someone can point out to me a non-Christian area of the planet, with reasonable population density and enough wealth to underwrite weapons production, where they *don't* invest their spare time in butchery for the ostensible sake of ideas. If not ideas about religion, then points of economic theory, or doctrines apparently supported by science. There hasn't quite been a war about evolutionary biology yet, but the brew of bad ideas in Nazism certainly drew on turn-of-the-twentieth-century speculations about racial difference which people at the time thought were Darwinian. Saviours, prophets, sages, poets, biologists, fashionable madmen, the voices of long-dead economists in the air: they all come in handy when we pink/sallow/brown/black monkeys need an alibi for cutting each other's throats.

But, but, but. Just invoking the HPtFtU is too easy. It may be true that without Christianity there would be other cruelties in the place of the Christian-committed ones, the inexhaustible fertility of the HPtFtU churning them out in endless forms most ugly: but the specific Christian cruelties are the ones we've actually got.

And beyond the category of shit that happens because people are just, fairly reliably, shitty, there are crimes and sorrows in human history that would not exist at all without Christianity. There are ills that would not be there without the specific Christian framing of human behaviour, without the presence of our specific story in human imagination. People who see Christianity as empowering horrors aren't generally just talking about the religion's failure to *stop* suffering, or about the lamentable gulf between what Christians say and what we do. They're talking about forms of suffering Christianity actually causes.

By now Christian history is very long and very diverse. After two thousand years, Christianity has existed in just about every conceivable human context. It has been the religion of dizzily plural societies and of stark human monocultures, of angry empires and of peaceful republics, of wealth and of poverty, of the desert and of the metropolis, of collectivism and individualism, of civilisations on the rise and at their peak and in decline and reduced to ruins and turned to bumps in the ground only an aerial photograph can find. It has been the religion of peasants who have seen no change in the world since their great-grandparents' time, and of nimble businessmen in skyscraper cities that didn't exist the year before. It has been quick and slow, crude and subtle, coercive and co-operative. It expresses different parts of its repertoire of possibilities in the different human niches where it has flourished: and also, it grows new pieces in each

172

of the places it finds itself. It has been incredibly adaptable. When I talk about 'the church' here, I don't mean any one organisation, I mean absolutely all of the congregations that descend from the group of Jesus's friends. The Pope's influential outfit in Rome, Brazilian storefront Pentecostalists dancing the samba, the Copts in Egypt, the Serbian Orthodox Patriarchate, Korean Presbyterians, the students of the Oral Roberts University: we're all the church of Christ. We're all, collectively, the *ecclesia*, 'the gathering together'.

Yet across all the variants, some things go wrong persistently. There's a set of failures which repeat, a group of malignant possibilities which come round again and again in different forms because they are failures generated close in to the unvarying core of the religion. They're Christianity's intimate disasters. They're the result of our HPtFtU acting on the story itself – or at least, on the way we understand the story, and what should follow from it. I can see four main areas of disaster.

Let's start with the worst. We are supposed to take the story of Jesus's death as God's spanner in the works of pain; an interruption by God to the cycle of human violence. But it is possible to treat it as an excuse for more pain, more violence. It all depends on whether we are willing to understand that the actors in the story, the people on the street and the soldiers, the Chief Priest and the governor, are just the front row of a crowd that also contains us. If we let ourselves see that the story is the story of everyone's culpability (and consequently of everyone's redemption) then we'll know that the inhabitants of Jerusalem in AD 33 who happen to be up at the front of the human crowd are not behaving in some exceptionally wicked way, they're just behaving like people. But this is hard. It's hard to accept your own destructiveness at the best of times, and the story raises the stakes to a dreadful level, offering us a bleeding image, written on a human body, of what it means for us and the world to go on as we usually do. The story asks us to abandon self-righteousness, there being the grimmest irony imaginable in it being the powers-that-be of the existing religion of the God of everything who co-operate unknowingly with the Romans to get God Himself killed. That's as difficult and uncomfortable as it always is, even if what lies beyond the difficulty is the ease of being fallible, and being forgiven. Watching Jesus stumble to Skull Hill requires work, requires sorrow, requires us not to look away from the spectacle of our world and ourselves. It's a lot easier for us than for him, but the nearest there comes to being a price for the utterly priceless, unpriced present God is trying to give us is that we need to be able to go on looking at the means by which He gives the gift. It's horrible: and all the while there is an easier option. We can stop seeing it as a story about all suffering and all guilt – a story of crucifixion which is dreadful because crucifixion is dreadful – and make it a story about a special shiny person, whose side we're all on as we listen, being abused by especially evil persons. Then what's wrong in the story is no longer that Jesus is being *crucified*, it's that *Jesus* is being crucified, lovely innocent Jesus. And, comfortably directed outwards, pity turns to anger, and anger turns to hate.

Since this is a general pattern, and the passion story can curdle to hatred in many contexts, quite a lot of different people can get hated. But there's been one ancient continuing target all the while. From the very beginning, the hate-inducing potential of the story was entangled in Christianity's relationship with its Jewish older sibling. In medieval Europe, Jesus's status as God incarnate was so entrenched in culture, he was so blazingly haloed and angel-attended in all the iconography, that it was virtually impossible for many people to imagine that he had ever been mistakeable for an ordinary man: so those who sent him to his death could not have been mistaken, or ordinarily culpable for an ordinary piece of realpolitik. They must have done so *because* of what he was, because they were the conscious enemies of God. Because in their pride and their alarming otherness and their sinister separateness they were deliberately siding against the good. Meanwhile, Jesus's own Jewishness, and his mother's, and his friends', disappeared from sight. Who gets hated? Those hooknosed Yids sneering at Our Lord in the painting; those other Yids who live three streets away, in the ghetto. Good Friday should be the day of all days in the Christian year when we are ashamed of even our tiniest and most necessary cruelties – seeing before us the image of their consequences. But instead, grotesquely, it was often the day for pogroms; a day of heightened emotions which could be resolved, for Christian mobs pouring out of churches, into a search for Jews to kill. Then Easter was celebrated with smoke and screams, and Christ re-crucified. The final catastrophe of European Jewry, in the twentieth century, wasn't just powered by religious anti-Semitism, but it played its part. This is the greatest shame of Christian history; the most disgusting misapplication possible of the story of com-passion unto death. My own church, and most of the other mainstream branches of the universal *ecclesia* too, now insists that on Good Friday we all of us in the building shout out 'Crucify him! Crucify him!', to re-mind us whodunnit, and that it wasn't Them. Unless the memory of the Holocaust fades in a way I don't an-ticipate, the specific danger of Christian anti-Semitism is much reduced. But there remains, always, the gener-al danger of pity turning to an anger sure it's on good's side: for it's righteous anger, in this world, with guilt pushed out of sight, that gets the crucifixions done.

There is another, more inward sense in which the story can be used as suffering's licence. We're supposed as Christians to go out and love recklessly, as God does. We're supposed to try and imitate Jesus in this, and to be prepared to follow love wherever it goes, knowing that there are no guarantees it'll be safe, or that the world will treat such vulnerability kindly. 'Take up your cross and follow me,' says Jesus in St Mark's Gospel, meaning: risk everything, even death. Take love's consequences. Don't be careful. He didn't mean: what I'm about to do needs doing again and again, by you. Once was enough for ever, and only God could do it anyway. He also didn't mean: go out, my dears, and hurt yourselves. But it is possible to read it that way, as a suggestion that we should embrace suffering by being enthusiastic about it, and there is a strand of self-directed violence in Christian history as a result, often committed by people who have a troubled or frightened relationship with their bodies anyway, and who are looking for a sanction to act on it. The lives of the saints contain cases that look suspiciously like anorexia, like self-mutilation, like terrified rejection of the bodily experiences of adulthood operating under cover of holiness. Christianity isn't a religion of self-harm, but self-harm can find a home in it, especially during one of the church's periodic panics about sexuality, when it can look as if the church is only willing to tolerate bodies on the most limited terms, and someone who doesn't like bodies at all can seem to be a spiritual virtuoso. This is not usually the same impulse, by the way, as the one that leads people to fast in Lent, or to become monks or nuns: there, what is being sacrificed is something the person enjoys, but which they are willing to give up in order to simplify their life, and to concentrate it around something they want and need (and enjoy) more. Monasteries, I'm glad to say, are full of hedonists. If this seems self-contradictory to you, then I would suggest you need to broaden your knowledge of human satisfactions.

Corrupting God's solidarity with human suffering into pretext, alibi, camouflage: that's our greatest failing. Then next in the roll-call of Christianity's most destructive failures comes our persistent desire to give grace a downgrade. We're supposed to see God's willingness to mend, to forgive, to absorb and remove guilt, as oceanic; a sea of love without limit, beating ceaselessly on the shores of our tiny island of caution and justice, always inviting us to look beyond, to begin again, to dare a larger and wilder and freer life. But it is possible to shrink it instead into something like a Get Out of Jail Free card, to be played by God only very occasionally in a game otherwise dominated by the same old rewards and punishments, human justice writ large all over the cosmos. Having begun with a powerful instruction to look beyond law, which human beings need, to see what else there is that we need too, Christianity has constantly tried to build new systems of law which can hold this thing we're told God wants us to notice. To hold it, to restrain it, to domesticate it, to bind it with rules, like Gulliver tied down by the ropes of the Lilliputians. Of course: because something kinder than fairness is, by definition, unfair, and once you take grace seriously it immediately threatens to produce scandalous unfairness in human terms. Jesus offered the very gentle, easy-way-in story of labourers who all get paid the same no matter when they turn up for work, but there are far harder, far more revolting consequences to grace. It is not for us to know who does and does not manage to accept forgiveness, but if the love really never stops, if God really does long for every lost soul, then in principle God regards as forgivable a whole load of stuff we really don't want forgiven, thank you. People who use airliners to murder thousands of office workers, people who strut about Norwegian summer camps stealing the lives of teenagers with careful shots to the head, people who drive over their gay neighbour in their pick-up truck and then reverse and do it again, people who torture children for sexual pleasure: God is apparently ready to rush right in there and give them all a hug, the bastard. We don't want that. We want justice, dammit, if not in this world then in the next. We want God's extra-niceness confined to deserving cases such as, for example, us, and a reliable process of judgement put in place which will ensure that the child-murderers are ripped apart with red-hot tongs.

So for most of its history, with varying degrees of certainty about whether the church really does have a bureaucratic grip on what happens after we're dead, Christianity has been in the hell business. You die; grace makes a momentary special-guest appearance for the defence courtesy of Jesus or, if he happens to be occupying the judge's seat just then, his mum; everyone admires God's classy but basically non-functional wish to be nice; and then you get exactly what you deserve. Hell, by contrast with God's niceness, is highly functional. It does lots and lots of work in human cultures. It operates as a deterrent, scaring the shit out of people who are contemplating doing bad things (and a lot of other people too, but hey, you can't have everything). It operates as a form of social control, since the misdemeanours that get you sent there somehow very often include cheeking your betters, asking awkward questions, embarrassing the powerful and engaging in unsightly degrees of class mobility. As if to make up for that, it also and simultaneously operates as a last-ditch form of social justice, promising that the malefactors of great wealth the law couldn't touch on earth will finally get theirs when they come before God's tribunal, where the clear-up rate for crimes is one hundred per cent. And, most weirdly, it operates on the side as a kind of theodicy, a peculiarly twisted attempt to solve the problem of pain. Imaginatively speaking, hell deals with suffering by doubling up on it, by coming up with something worse, alongside which anthrax and toothache and Colonel Gaddafi don't look so bad. Hell drowns out this-worldly suffering in horror. Alongside the world, it lays in imagination this other domain which is all horror, all the time, without our world's mixture of qualities, and without the finiteness which ensures that, in life, even the worst things end. The idea being that here suffering is finally put on a proper basis, with proper moral causation in place. In hell, rocks never fall randomly out of an empty sky and break your skull. In hell, it only happens if you deserve it. In hell, the bad things only happen to guaranteed bad people.

But of course hell's handy little bundle of social utility – unlike the grace of God – comes at a cost. Hell makes God Himself a torturer. It produces grotesque distortions in what we'd have to mean when we talk about His 'love'. If love can be manifested in scooping out the eyeballs of unrepentant criminals over and

over again for all eternity, then (if I may refer you
back to Chapter Four) it instantly fails the John Stuart
Mill test of being recognisable as the phenomenon humans call by the same name. Moreover – guaranteed
bad people? What has happened to the central Christian recognition that we're *all* bad people, in need of
mercy? Somehow, in hell, limitless compassion acquires
very definite limits: limits so tightly drawn that in the
end it becomes inescapably clear that the whole con-
trivance, besides being repellently sadistic in itself, is
blatantly incompatible with the primary thing Christianity believes about God, and must in fact be another
of the shadows of our failure, another vengeful projection of the HPtFtU of Christian humans, rather than
part of the furniture of God's universe.

And here I have good news for once. Hell is still popular – just look at the way the tabloids invoke it, whenever
they need a way to describe evil that won't decompose
into touchy-feely social-work-speak – but not with actual
Christians, any more. Crazy avant-gardists that we are,
we went ahead and decided to do without it some time
ago. The majority of us have not believed in it for several
generations. It isn't because we're wimpy modernisers
who can't stomach the more scaly and brimstone-rich aspects of our inheritance. It's because, from the beginning, hell conflicted with much more basic aspects of the
religion, and our collective understanding finally caught
up with the fact. Those posters you occasionally see on
buses and rail platforms threatening you with un-
quenchable fire come from a tiny faction of head-

bangers. We don't like them either. (I myself would rather have the atheist bus any day.) I promise this is really true. No more hell! It's official! The smiliness of Christians may be creepy for other reasons, but we are not, I swear, biding our time and waiting for everyone who disagrees with us to get slung into the pit. We are not smiling because we are waiting patiently for you lot to fry. Honest. Except in miniscule enclaves, the centuries are over in which the threat of hell was wielded to ensure conformity, passivity and deference; in which it terrified and tormented the living; in which it was used to justify the cruelties of earthly law; in which it served as a narrow, frightened, legalistic refusal of the generosity we were supposed to be celebrating.

While we're talking about law, let's talk about power as well: the next area of disaster. Quite a lot of people imagine a version of Christian history that comes with a moment of decisive downfall where power is concerned. Usually they point to the 330s AD, when Constantine the Great made Christianity the official religion of the Roman empire. No more innocent sect; from then on, a branch of the state, wielding the weapons of the state to enforce an intolerant monopoly. Goodbye, the holy impossibilism of the preacher from Galilee; hello, bishops sending the police to heretics' houses. I don't buy it myself – not, at any rate, the idea that power in itself has poisoned Christianity. There *is* a characteristic and persistent Christian failure where power is concerned, but it's much more specific. Power as such is not optional. Having a relationship with it of some kind, whether wielding it or being subject to it, comes as standard in human societies. For the church, relating to power one way or another is a necessary consequence of operating in the world, or rather of trying to straddle two worlds: of trying to witness to an unconditional love while also doing what is needful to go on existing in the world of conditions. It's a paradox. In order to still be there tomorrow saying, 'Take no thought for tomorrow', the church has to think about tomorrow.* The very early church, and quite possibly Jesus too, expected that the problem would solve itself shortly, because the world was about to end. It didn't, and instead it became clear that Christians were going to have to build and maintain and bargain as well as living out God's impractical foolishness.

Given that inevitability, none of the choices available for the Christian relationship with power are uncomplicated. All of them are compromises of some description, and all of them lead to culpability of some kind. You can refuse the violence all power depends

---

* Perhaps this is the place to try and lay to rest the bizarre idea that my own church, the Church of England, is 'rich'. Somehow, the people who say it is only ever look at the C. of E.'s assets, never its liabilities. Wealth is assets minus liabilities, and the church's income from its investments is outweighed, and then some, by its bills for salaries and pensions. This is true even with maximum use of volunteers, and fewer and fewer paid priests, and each priest covering more and more parishes, and longer and longer gaps between priests in the parishes when they move on elsewhere. The church's portfolio is valued in the (low) billions, but that's because it operates on a very large scale. Disaggregate the billions, and you find that on a local level the reality everywhere is one of penny-pinching, and continuous fund-raising just to keep the roof on the thousands of ancient churches. It takes all

on, as some sects of Christians have always done, and
be pacifists like the Quakers or the Amish, but then

---

the running we can do to stay in the same place. It's not as if the assets
could be liquidated, anyway. They aren't being held for their cash
value, and they don't belong to us to dispose of. The purpose of the
church's money is not to make money, but to contrive for it to go on being true that the church is there whenever it is needed. Everywhere
in England is in a parish. Everyone in England has a priest they can
go to. In the unlikely event that a heartbroken Richard Dawkins wants
help with his HPtFtU, there will be somebody tired but willing in
North Oxford whose responsibility it is to offer him an inexpensive
digestive biscuit and a cup of milky tea, and to listen to him for as
long as it takes. Meanwhile, the personnel who do this are not exactly
coining it: certainly not in comparison with the rewards available to
those who write 'brave' anti-religious bestsellers, or to comedians being 'iconoclastic'. A parish priest aged fifty, driving frantically
between her five or six leaking churches, burying people and marry-
ing people and sitting with the dying and serving as the messenger
across all of the contemporary divides and keeping faith with both
hope and despair and trying to ease where she can the weight of sorrow and cruelty, earns about £22,500 a year, about as much as a recently qualified nurse. She gets a house, which is not to be sniffed at,
but it vanishes at retirement, of course. (And although there are still
a few nice big houses in the country, the cash-strapped Church Com-
missioners have sold off almost all the pretty architecture for what it
will fetch. 'The Old Rectory' is an address for a stockbroker.) A bishop, managing while trying to be more than a manager, and represent-
ing the faith to a world inclined to believe it's all a cover for bigotry and
kiddy-fiddling, and contriving to uphold a carved medieval mountain which is always trying to fall down, earns £39,000, slightly less
than the salary of a long-serving police sergeant. The Archbishop of
Canterbury – our overburdened intellectual with the beard, doomed
to please nobody – earns £72,000, slightly more than the salary (before expenses) of an ordinary MP, vanishingly less than the income
of any chief executive of any organisation doing anything anywhere
in the private sector. Nobody in our time ever joins the church to get
rich. There is ancient splendour, yes, but it's all in trust. You might
consider these figures the next time you see someone stuck on auto-
sneer about the 'wealth' and 'power' of the clergy. Especially if they
themselves have a job in financial services.

you end up tacitly depending, for protection and civil order, on those who do get their hands dirty. You become power's free riders, taking the benefits without paying the price. You can withdraw into a monastic pocket civilisation, where family and biology's obligations are suspended, along with the state's, but then somebody else, again, has to have and raise the children, and make the world safe enough for them. You can make your refusal of power violent in itself, and fight a perfectionist guerrilla war for your vision of the kingdom, but what if you win? What if your militia of Anabaptists or Fifth Monarchy Men enters the filthy city victorious, and you suddenly have to keep the power station running, and put burglars on trial? The necessities of the world keep imposing themselves.

Or you can come to terms with power in some form, allying with it or supporting it or participating in it or trying to take it over; and then the other end of the paradox, the other horn of the dilemma, begins to dig into you. For though Christianity will function, more or less, as an ideology of power, it never does so easily and conveniently, like the law-giving religions. It never does so without an awkward residue being left over. You can tell the gospel as a story about authority, if you choose to – Jesus passing on the power to speak for God to human deputies, whether St Peter and his heirs (Catholic version), pious emperors of Constantinople and Moscow (Orthodox), or evangelists leading prayer breakfasts at the White House (Protestant) – but then what do you do with the insistence that God sees the world upside down, from the vant-age point of failure, from our gutters not our palaces? What do you do with His endless alarm about loss, and His indifference to possession? What do you do about Christ's preference for having dinner with the rogues and the screw-ups and the enemies of public order? No matter how hunky-dory the authorities of some supposedly Christian set-up declare things to be, the church is always nurturing the seeds of a critique. We can't help it. The critique is always there in the story, and as we value the story, we have to keep the critique of power available.

And this is Christianity's saving grace where power is concerned. Literally. For the source of our shame, the source of the general pattern of sorrow power has created in Christian history, is not power itself, but confidence about power. Certainty about power. Op-timism about power, of a kind that contradicts Jesus's grimly kind lack of faith in our chances of managing righteousness. We are supposed to believe that hu-man attempts at perfection will mean a nice slab on top, worms underneath; but it is possible, with a bit of squinting, to imagine that because we're Christians, our projects might somehow share in God's freedom from the HPtFtU. Then power, rather than being just another medium in which we're sure to struggle and blunder as we try to articulate the vision of grace, might itself be sanctified. Christian power might be holy, and be exercised successfully for holy purposes, without irony, without humility, without doubt. As always seems to be the case, the vainglorious certainty that the HPtFtU can be excluded from some area of human experience only serves to invite it straight in around the back, to romp around fucking things up on the grand scale. When Christians try to exercise power as if it were God doing it, cruelty and suffering and tyranny follow swiftly. In short order, we get the steely-eyed monks of the Inquisition trying to drag the Moors and Jews of Spain into perfect orthodoxy, one fingernail at a time; we get the theocrats of Protestant New England hanging Quakers and dispensing scarlet letters; we get holy war, with weapons of ever-increasing sophistication. We get Guantánamo. We get Abu Ghraib. We get waterboarding. Yet all the while, something nags. To Christians, power rubs and chafes, even when it's necessary. You may think that it's the essence of religion to believe that some human agenda or other has divine backing, there being no other source of agendas *except* humanity, but our sky fairy is an uncooperative one. It manifests as a voice comparing the kingdom to twenty different impractical, unplannable, ungovernable things. In the heat of some dreadful surge of certainty, we may manage to drown the voice out for a while. But it always comes back in the end, reminding us that power is not in itself what we are supposed to be hoping for. It is not the medium in which the kingdom can be realised. Unfortunately, before 'in the end' arrives, there has often been time for us to fill the prisons and bless the armoured divisions.

Nor does the church need to have wielded direct

civil authority to do harm to the flourishing of the lives within its reach. The power of perception is considerable too, the power to mould cultural judgements. Here is the fourth and last of the areas of persistent damage for which Christianity is to blame: our recurring tendency to give religious sanction to whatever is small-'c' conservative in a society, at the expense of everybody who falls outside the conservative definition of what's good and natural. We are supposed to be the universal harbour for the guilty, an organisation in which no one claims to look at anyone else from the higher ground of virtue. We are supposed to be on the side of goodness in the sense that we need it, not that we are it. But it is possible to see the church, instead, as virtue's tribe, as a new version of the old self-satisfied Us, with the edge of the church standing as the edge of familiarity, the edge of the comfortable, and fusing in imagination with the anthropologically inevitable boundary between the clean and the dirty, the safe and the frightening. Then whatever is inside the tribal boundary begins to seem good because it is inside, and whatever is outside begins to seem wicked because it is outside.

This produces a moral map of the world where virtue is determined by labels rather than by actions: by what your label says you are, not by what you do. Given the universality of the HPtFtU, it follows that a lot of everyday spite and unpleasantness, and worse, is going to go on under the label of insiderish goodness, and may well be given cover, consciously or unconsciously, by other insiders who believe that they are defending the dignity of the Christian label. Or even that they are defending goodness itself – which is the same thing, according to the insider/outsider map. If your priority is to maintain the axiomatic wonderfulness of Christian marriage, then you may not want to listen very hard to news of wife-battering, marital rape and petty domestic tyranny. If your priority is to proclaim the axiomatic wonderfulness of the Christian family, then you may not want to pay much attention to stories of children abused. If your priority is to revere the axiomatic wonderfulness of the priesthood, then you may not want to give much credence to the whispers about Father Stephen and the altar boys. You won't mean, by any of these acts of deliberate ignorance, to *approve* of the ills in question. You just deny that they can be happening; and since they do happen, people being people, your silence helps them to go on happening. Your preference for the bright-coloured map gives them permission to continue. And to the victims, seeing how the goodness and holiness of what hurts them is constantly affirmed, it can seem as if God Himself approves the harm. 'The earth is heavy with His presence,' says the psalm. Intolerably heavy, crushingly heavy, if you are taught that God is in the pinning weight you must not complain of.

And as for attitudes towards those seen as being on the dirty outside of the tribe, especially if their difference is frightening in some way, especially if their difference has to do with sexuality: oh my. It is of course an illusion to imagine that the dykes and the queers and the trannies are all safely locked out there in the outer darkness rather than being in here with us, in fact *being* us, but that's what the corrupting little map of virtue suggests, and quite a lot of those who are conducting my own church's stumbling rearguard action against gay rights seem to feel that they are defending a fortress of traditional behaviour against hordes of drag queens on crack. The record of the church here is, frankly, rubbish. We are supposed, always, to be trying to love what we don't like or understand or want to touch; we are supposed to be taking as little notice of boundaries to love as we believe God does. We are supposed to be looking at each other in guilty brotherhood and sisterhood. We are *not* supposed to be assigning guilt according to who does what with whom. Categories of clean and dirty belong in the law-religions, not in Christianity. Where consenting adults are concerned, we ought to be as uninterested in lists of forbidden sexual acts as we are in lists of forbidden foods. 'Objectively disordered', my arse. The disorder is in our hearts. Sexual sins matter, all right – where selves touch so closely, what more fertile field could there be for the HPtFtU? – but any of us can commit them, and we usually do, taking hold of each other coldly, carelessly, mockingly, exploitatively, angrily, as if the other or our own self were a convenient object rather than flesh requiring our recognition and our tenderness. Sexual guilt, like every other kind, is distributed across the entire human race.

As we've seen, the founding story of Christianity is astonishingly unbothered about it. Jesus didn't think it was worth picking it out in particular to talk about it. Yet Christians seem to be intensely and continuously bothered. In other areas of life, dealing with other kinds of difference and other hierarchies of status and privilege, like those of race or class or caste, we have managed at times over the last century to live up to the emancipatory promise of our faith. The Civil Rights movement in the United States being a proud case in point, where Christian theology and the Christian critique of power helped a dispossessed people to demand freedom.* When it comes to the oppression of women and sexual minorities, not so much. Far from giving any kind of emancipatory lead, the church has struggled along behind, always late, always reluctant, accepting with palpable difficulty and discomfort liberations that became normal outside the church a generation earlier. My own church digs in its feet about women being bishops, about gay men being bishops, about same-sex marriage and adoption by gay couples.

---

* According to Christopher Hitchens, the Reverend Martin Luther King cannot be counted to the credit of the religion. 'In no real as opposed to nominal sense, then, was he a Christian.' He was *too good*, you see. The non-violence, the humility – utterly incompatible with Christianity's proven wickedness. While we consider the rigorous logic of this position, let's all sing that great Civil Rights anthem 'Eyes on the Prize'. *Put my hand on the gospel plough* [Luke 9.62], *won't take nothing for my journey now* [Mark 6.8] . . . *The only thing we did was wrong, was staying in the wilderness too long* [Matthew 4.1–8], *keep your eyes on the prize* [1 Corinthians 9.24–5] *and hold on* [1 Thessalonians 5.21] . . . No, nothing Christian there.

It constantly contrives to signal that it rates the unhappiness of the traditionally-minded higher in the scale of priorities than any injustice or violence or hatred suffered by those whom tradition excludes. It gives the impression that it would be preferable if homosexuality ceased to exist, or failing that, if homosexuals would all remain silent and invisible and (naturally) celibate all their lives, tidily locked away in self-hating self-denial. Meanwhile, it maintains warm, chatty relationships with sister churches around the world which (Uganda) advocate the death penalty for gay sex, or (Nigeria) hold that there is no such thing as sexual orientation, just individuals giving in to sodomitical wickedness. It's no wonder people conclude that Christianity is intrinsically homophobic and misogynistic.

However, there is a misapprehension here. The everyday moral consensus of the western European and North American world has shifted sharply on the subjects of sexuality and gender roles over the last fifty years. It's been a swift, epochal social change. And because the church has been slow to participate in it, and was committed before it (with only a very few exceptions) to the pre-feminist and pre-Stonewall understanding of what was right 'n' proper, many people now assume that the church must be bigoted on principle. They presume that the bigoted world of the past was bigoted because the church then had the power to enforce its bigoted principle, and is no longer bigoted because the church has lost the power to impose it. Surely the Christian scriptures must contain somewhere the announcement that the Westboro Baptist Church puts on its delightful placards, God Hates Fags. Obviously, they think, mainstream churchy types are a bit more circumspect about expressing it than the Westboro nutcases, seeing that it doesn't go down very well these days, but just look at the news, just look at the way the churches writhe and cringe when they're asked to follow the equality laws. It's the same thing. The Bible teaches hate. They try to hide it now, but it's too late; that old tyrannical pleasure-prohibiting stuff has lost its grip on us. We're off to dance the night away at the roller-disco, daddy-o, wearing hot-pants and smooching whom we please, and you can't stop us, you sad old religious nobodies. We're free! Free at last, free at last, thank God Almighty we're free at last. (Whoops, wrong liberation struggle.)

But there is no such principle. Christian homophobia and misogyny do not proceed from an instruction in our Big Black How-To Book of Hate. (And in any case the Bible is a library, not a manual.) They are a consequence of the church's immersion in the prejudices, assumptions and habits of the world before the change, formed by that world as much as forming it. More broadly, they are a consequence of the way Christianity always exists in a culture, and grows to fill whatever human niche it finds itself in. At its essential heart, it is very simple and radical, and it does not actually require most of the heterogeneous material that gets gathered up along with the gathering of the people into each local crazy-paved caddis-larva assemblage. But the difference between the bits that are core and the bits that are periphery is not always very apparent from where a particular person, or a particular society, is standing. A lot of stuff gets hoovered up,* including, in each society, an instinctual semi-conscious sense of what constitutes the unchanging part of human experience. The part that doesn't ebb and flow with fashion and the weather. The part that is bedrock. I talked earlier about the church giving supernatural sanction to small-'c' conservatism, and that's what this is. Not large-'C' Conservatism, with a philosophy and a programme; not a rule, not a principle, not a judgement for all times and seasons. Just a preference for what seems old, settled, permanent, with respect to (relative to) one particular time and place. Tradition varies. The conservatism of an elderly French peasant is different from the conservatism of a twenty-five-year-old Californian lawyer, which is different again from the conservatism of a Nigerian market-stall matriarch who thinks her daughter-in-law is a hussy on the make. The common link is a kind of poetics of order; an expectation that the ultimate (but invisible) solidity of God can be found in, is reflected in, whatever in daily life seems most

---

* Philosophy and cosmology, for example, as well as food rituals, dress codes, laws of inheritance and views on the appropriate level of interest rates. This is how the medieval Latin church finds itself temporarily committed to the metaphysics of Aristotle and the bibbity-bobbity clockwork solar system of Ptolemy.

solid. Which means, the way the world worked when I first learned the world. Which means, the old ways, whatever they were. This plays a much larger role in Christian hostility to changes in sexual behaviour than does any positive adherence to, for instance, the sexual code in the Book of Leviticus. (We don't obey the twiddly behavioural bits of ancient Jewish law at all, in fact, grace having replaced them.) My own church contains actual homophobes here and there, of course, but it is dragging its feet primarily because it was so deeply acculturated to the world before the change. It had bound itself to the habits and outlook of that world, and those in the church who are the right age now remember the order of things in the 1950s as the old stuff, the sanctified stuff, the solid stuff, from which it is frightening and dangerous to move on. Naturally this isn't just a phenomenon that affects perceptions of sexuality, or that applies to that one generation of church members. Similar patterns of time-lag explain why the Church of England also preserves, as if in aspic, pockets of 1980s-style anti-racism, and a number of 1970s-style beardy lefties. Cough the Archbishop of Canterbury cough.

Obviously this is not much substantial comfort, if you're being gay-bashed outside a pub, and the church is wringing its hands and going oo-er-I-feel-your-pain *to the people kicking your head in*. But it has implications for the future. It strongly suggests that the church will get there in the end. Slow and late and pathetically reluctant, it will eventually allow the central commandment we *have* got, to love our neighbours as we love ourselves, to overrule the poetry of custom; and the church will reconfigure, at snail-like speed, for a new social reality. By then, however, social reality is sure to have changed again. There is no 'in the end' for human societies. So the implication is not that the church has to make its way through a finite menu of accommodations to social justice, after which it will have sorted itself out and become an institution in good order, which enlightened people can be glad to have around. There will always be more change needed. There always has been more change needed. The process is never-ending. For ever and ever, in any possible future, the church will always be adjusting imperfectly to new times, and then un-adjusting again later, also imperfectly, with occasional lucky breaks where grace, crackling onwards through history, helps us to a sudden generosity. The church will always be clumsy and time-lagged and complicit in the corruptions of its times. The slowness of the church will sometimes exhibit a kind of wisdom, protecting what is beautiful and vulnerable in our inheritance, insulating us from inane enthusiasm for change as such, guarding us against the illusion that we can renew ourselves at will; but there will always be costs exacted for it too, in human needs recognised too sluggishly, in injustices scandalously tolerated. There will never come a year zero after which we are pure. We're the league of the guilty, after all, not the league of the shortly-to-become-good. We are a work in progress.

We will always be a work in progress. We will always fail, and it will always matter.

And the same applies to our other intimate disasters: to all the patterns of harm that spread from our abuse of our story, from our falls from grace into punishment, from our temptation to believe we can be God's holy regents on the earth. On they roll. On they will roll, no doubt, in new forms for as long as there are Christians, people being what we are, the HPtFtU being what it is. If we waited for the church to clean up, if we waited for the church to be nothing but good, to do nothing but good, we would wait for ever.

So we don't wait. We don't, in fact, believe the church is precious because it is good or does good or because it may do good in future. We care about its behaviour, but we don't believe that its muddled and sometimes awful record is the only truth about it. We believe that the church is precious because it embodies something that the HPtFtU in general and our sins of complicity in particular cannot destroy. Something which already exists now, despite our every failure, and which consequently always has existed for Christians, right through all the dark centuries when slavery and tyranny governed the world, and the church too, and the modern idea of rights was not yet even imaginable. When the abbot was a thug who got the abbey from the thug his brother who was king, when the bishop did send the bootboys round, when famine raged and the clergy stayed fat, this other thing stayed true. Was already true. Didn't have to be waited for.

For us, you see, the church is not just another institution. It's a failing but never quite failed attempt,
by limited people, to perpetuate the unlimited generosity of God in the world. It's built, of all things, on
a pun. I said 'embodies' and the word is exact. The
church is a body that wants to be a body. That is, it's
a *corpus*, a *corporation*, a 'body' of people in the sense
of being a gathered crowd of them, which aspires to
be, to carry on from, to keep alive and present and
breathing, the literal *corporeal* body of Jesus, equipped
with two arms and two legs and probably the beard and
quite possibly the bad teeth, in first-century Palestine.
You do not need to tell us that this is impossible. We
know. But we are committed to the impossible anyway,
with our ideals of behaviour that only the God of
everything can manage, and our efforts to possess a
state of being which is only even visible in this world
in glimpses, in metaphors, in temporary comparisons.
We're used to trying and failing at the impossible.
And now and again gaining a piece of the possible
we wouldn't have had and wouldn't have known was
possible, if we hadn't been trying for the impossible
beyond it. So the church, we say, is the body of Christ:
another comparison with a truth flickering in and out
of sight in it. The church is what Christ is doing in the
world, nowadays. This is not the same thing as saying
that the church is magically good no matter what, or
that good intentions cancel lousy results. (No balance
sheet, remember?) It's not the basis for an excuse, but
if anything, for self-accusation. It's a reason for us to

be harder on ourselves rather than easier. But it's also a reason for never quite losing hope, never letting go of the conviction that, in its stumbling way, the church faces toward grace. That it exists, like Christ, in order to be a channel by which mending enters the world; a mending which, thank God, does not depend on the success of human virtue, individual or collective, but on what breathes and shines through us if we let it.

The church is one of the answers to the question of where Christ is since he left us at the end of the story, alive but no longer committed to, limited to, the physical life of the one man Yeshua. Where is he? Here. His hands are our hands now, the only hands he's got. My hands, typing this. Your hands, whenever you push with them at the dire engine of our history, to try to shift it, just a little bit, in the direction of kindness. His face is every face that passes in the street. He's the junkie playing the whistle by the supermarket. He's the tired-looking Somali woman with the pushchair. He's everyone you care for and everyone you distrust. Unlimited love having once entered into limited us, it's here for good, apparent to us or invisible depending on the light, depending on our willingness to see. Humanity glimmers with God's presence.

And he is most specifically of all *here*, we believe, when we follow the instructions he gave at dinner the night before he died. Every Sunday morning, in all the church's human niches, from downtown Isfahan to downtown Manhattan, in places of great wealth and comfort and in cities under bombardment, on every

continent including Antarctica and once I believe on
the moon, we hold again a stylised version of the original Passover meal in Jerusalem. There is bread, there
is wine. We bless them using one of the Passover prayers. We break the bread, we pour the wine into a cup.
We repeat Jesus's words from the story. This is my
body. This is my blood. And then for us the bread,
made unmysteriously from wheat, and the wine, made
unmysteriously from grapes, are different. There has
been a change in their meaning. For some of us, the
material bread and material wine have altered (on a
tiny domestic scale, with crumbs and dregs and
washing-up) in the same way that the material world
was altered by having its creator within it. Right there
on the table, the set of the world once more contains
itself as a member; once more, a peculiar knot has
been tied in the fabric of existence. For others of us,
the change of meaning is made by the material world
aligning itself to form a sign of what began happening
once in Jerusalem long ago, and (the sign reminds us)
is still happening now. Either way, the change puts the
same strange burden on our imagination and our understanding when we do what we do next, and eat the
bread, and drink the wine. We're eating God. We're
eating Jesus. The body that wants to be a body is eating
the body it wants to be. The pun multiplies. 'O taste
and see', the choir may be singing, if it's the altar of
a cathedral we're filing towards to take our bite and
our swallow of the meal. The tasting is literal: tongues,
teeth, gullet and intestines are all involved. The God

of everything is demonstrating again his gross indifference to good taste in the other, polite, little-finger-extended sense. Because it's inescapable: this is an act of sacred cannibalism, in symbolic form. The Romans, used to temples where the literal blood of animals flowed, passed round rumours of the vile stuff Christians got up to on a Sunday, and perhaps it's too easy for us now to soothe away into familiarity the language we use. Perhaps there ought to be a hint of repulsion, of taboos overridden, when we sup the red stuff in the chalice, to keep us reminded of where our sign is pointing: which is towards Skull Hill, and the human body on the cross there. We aren't just eating Jesus. We're eating his death. We eat and we drink because we desire monstrosity's end, but the sacrament carries us into the monstrous, through the monstrous, to get us there, just as the story we tell only arrives at hope by way of tragedy. The meanings of the bread and the wine line up along a bloody corridor, as barbarous as the barbarous world God is working on, and at the end of the corridor, once we have accepted the strange and frightening gift we are being given, there is forgiveness. We eat the bread, we drink the wine, to be joined to the act by which forgiveness came. We eat the end of cruelty and shame. We eat amnesty for whatever the particular load of the HPtFtU was that we brought to the dinner table. We eat the rejoicing that this one time, in spite of all sorrow, the world's weight was flipped over and turned to joy. We eat grace.

And that's what the church is for. Forget about

saints, popes, bishops, monks, nuns, processions, statues, music, art, architecture, vicarage tea parties, telethons, snake-handling, speaking in tongues, special hats. All of that stuff * can be functional in its time and its place, can do things sometimes to inch forward the work of love, but it's all secondary, it's all flummery, it's all essentially decorative compared to this. We eat the bread. We drink the wine. We feel ourselves forgiven. And, feeling that, we turn from the table to try to love the world, and ourselves, and each other.

If you come to a parish church in England after the service, what you will see is a (small) crowd of elderly people, middle-aged people and young families, balancing biscuits and cups of coffee in one hand as we do crowd control on the children with the other, and making slightly awkward conversation about the weather, holidays, cricket scores, the news, the progress of flowers and vegetables. We don't necessarily have very much in common with each other, by all the usual standards. We're embarrassed, probably. (After all, this is England.) And yet that's not all that is going on. We're also celebrating the love-feast. Our hearts are in our eyes as we look at each other. We are engaged in the impossible experiment of trying to see each other the way God sees us. That is, as if we were all precious beyond price, for reasons quite independent of any of the usual cues for attraction we apes jump to recognise: status, charisma, beauty, confidence, wealth, wisdom, authority.

---

* OK, I'm not sure about the snake-handling.

It's an impersonal kind of loving, looked at one way, since it doesn't ask what we ourselves want or like. Looked at another way, it's very, very personal indeed, because its focus is all on the other, all on what they're actually like, not as we can hope to know it, but as a loving sustainer could, who reads them illusionlessly from within, and delights in them anyway. It's a kind of vision you fall out of again very fast, even with discipline, even with your best try at selfless attention, but something is retained, something in the trick of it is catching and gets laid down as habit. Some ground is gained, somehow. And it's a mode of pleasure, too. There they are – there we are – to be enjoyed, in a way that overlaps with the way you can enjoy the people in a novel, whether or not they fall comfortably within what you thought, before you started reading, were the natural bounds of your sympathies, your preferences, your interests. Grace makes us better readers of each other. We don't know, each of us, what the others needed forgiving for, and we never will, but we know they were forgiven, as we were, and for whole moments we manage to see with calm, kind ease. Though we are many, we say, we are one body, because we all share in one bread.

And then we fail. And we try again, and fail again, and go on trying. Always failing, always hoping to fail better, because we know that it is through loving the resistant, muddled, tricky, intricate, fascinating, stained fabric of this world – this only world – that it begins to glint with the possibility of the kingdom. Or the republic! By all means, think of it as the republic of heaven. There is no king here, except the king we see in each other's faces, and we're all fallible; none of us is any better than the rest. What better citizens for a republic could there be?

8

Consequences

What does it feel like to feel yourself forgiven? I can only speak for myself, but, speaking for myself: surprising. Just as it comes from a direction you hadn't considered, viewing your life from an angle you hadn't expected, it also comes with a sensation that isn't necessarily one of conventional release or relief. In my experience, it's like toothache stopping because a tooth has been removed. It has the numb surprisingness of something that hurt not being there any more. You explore the space where it was, and you feel slightly changed, slightly self-alienated. Something has been reconfigured a bit. There's some unfamiliarity close in. You're glad, of course, that it doesn't hurt, but you can find that you almost miss the familiar signal of your own distress, especially since the memory of how much it hurt fades fast, and it's difficult to go on rejoicing positively over an absence. You may find, in fact, that you feel a sly temptation to restore the status quo ante, by going out and doing again the thing you needed forgiving for, whatever it was. After all, you've just discovered it was survivable, that there was a route out of desperation and self-reproach; and this way you won't have to deal with the unsettling open-endedness of being changed. Is there a possibility of, as it were, moral hazard, in which the removal of negative consequences makes it perversely *easier* to do the thing again? Oh yes. Humans can fuck up anything. The mafioso taking himself to confession after every hit is only an extreme case of a familiar pattern. Grace is the answer to our abuses of ourselves and each other, but grace itself can be abused. It's hard to wait and stay in the tremulous uncertain state grace puts us in, not knowing what its changes may mean, not knowing where they may take us. Forgiveness has no price we need to pay, but it exposes our illusions of control. Forgiveness is not flattering. Forgiveness reminds us that our masks are masks. Forgiveness starts something, if we let it. Forgiveness comes with an invitation to find out what else we may become that we hadn't suspected. Forgiveness carries you into new territory. Forgiveness is disconcerting.

But then so much of the rest of faith is disconcerting too. Every step of it requires you to embrace risk in some way or other, from the risk that you're getting the nature of the universe absurdly wrong, to the risk of putting aside your dignity and signing up to a picture of yourself as pratfall-prone and self-subverting, rather than the proud master of your destiny. Supposing you do it, though – supposing you take the risk, and it happens that you follow (of all the pathways to faith there are) the path this book has described. Supposing that in one of life's recurrent encounters with bleakness you acknowledge the crack in everything; and supposing you find that you do feel, in the great silence that answers when you ask for help, that something is speak-

ing; and supposing you make your way through the
shoals of theodicy; and supposing the story moves you,
moves you enough for you to give it your provisional assent; and supposing you nervously join the company of
other assenters, and eat the bread and drink the wine;
and supposing you tentatively begin to try to walk the
walk of faith, pratfalls and all – what then? What follows? Where does this new experiment in indignity lead
you? What does it commit you to?

Early on in this I compared beginning to believe to
falling in love, and the way that faith settles down in a
life is also very like the way that the first dizzy-intense
phase of attraction settles (if it does) into a relationship.
Rapture develops into routine, a process which keeps
its customary doubleness where religion is concerned.
It's both loss and gain together, with excitement dwin-
dling and trust growing; like all human ties, it constricts
at the same time as it supports, ruling out other choices
by the very act of being a choice. And so as with any com-
mitment, there are times when you notice the limit on
your theoretical freedom more than you feel what the
attachment is giving you, and then it tends to be habit,
or the awareness of a promise given, that keeps you trying. God makes an elusive lover. The unequivocal blaze
of His presence may come rarely or not at all, for years
and years – and in any case cannot be commanded, will
not ever present itself tamely to order. He-doesn't-exist-
the-bastard may be much more your daily experience
than anything even faintly rapturous. And yet, and yet.
He may come at any moment, when and how you least

expect it, and that somehow slightly colours every moment in the mass of moments when he doesn't come.
And grace, you come to recognise, never stops, whether
you presently feel it or not. You never stop doubting –
how could you? – but you learn to live with doubt and
faith unresolved, because unresolvable. So you don't
keep digging the relationship up to see how its roots are
doing. You may have crises of faith but you don't, on the
whole, ask it to account for itself philosophically from
first principles every morning, any more than you subject your relations with your human significant other to
daily cost–benefit analysis. You accept it as one of the
givens of your life. You learn from it the slow rewards of
fidelity. You watch as the repetition of Christmases and
Easters, births and deaths and resurrections, scratches
on the linear time of your life a rough little model of His
permanence. You discover that repetition itself, curi-
ously, is not the enemy of spontaneity, but maybe even
its enabler. Saying the same prayers again and again, pa-
cing your body again and again through the set movements of faith, somehow helps keep the door ajar
through which He may come. The words may strike you
as ecclesiastical blah nine times in ten, or ninety-nine
times in a hundred, and then be transformed, and then
have the huge fresh wind blowing through them into
your little closed room. And meanwhile you make faith
your vantage point, your habitual place to stand. And
you get used to the way the human landscape looks from
there: reoriented, reorganised, different.

It has not had meaning drained out of it, that land-

scape. Or variety. Or endless interesting human par-
ticularity. It has not become the mere illustration to
some abstract proposition about the nature of people.
If anything it has become solider and finer-grained
and more intricately itself, an endless spur to further
curiosity. God is not distinct from human beings for
Christians, remember. We are not supposed to look
away from people towards Him. In fact, we are commanded not to. We are supposed to look for Him in
each other's faces, and to love specifically, concretely,
with the largest and most generous and of course most
curious sense of the other we can possibly manage. God
is both into exclusivity and not. There are to be no other gods but Him: no flirtations with Matching Curtains
and Being Well Endowed, or their harder-to-recognise
present-day counterparts, our little ad hoc modern
idols of wealth and power. Nothing is to be worshipped
except the God of everything, who doesn't need worship and doesn't require it of us (though we may offer
it if we want, from the same motion of the heart that
makes us stretch out our hands on mountaintops). On
the other hand, everything is pretty damn plural, and
neither God's love for us nor ours for God is supposed to displace other loves. It is supposed, in fact,
to encourage and even sanctify them. It is supposed
to send us out, reverent and eager and crazy-curious,
full of passion for each other's minds, hearts, souls,
bodies, wanting to recreate as best we can in miniature
some fraction of the absolute and inimitable love behind everything.

209

But that same curiosity reveals, and keeps on reveal-
ing, the crack in everything. It's a messed-up world
inhabited by messed-up people. The HPtFtU is universal. Our destructiveness is a truth about us just as
basic as our capacity for love. Our loves are always going to be checked, complicated, limited, compromised,
corrupted, undermined, reversed by the rest of what
we are. If you accept this, the refusal to admit it in contemporary culture starts to look silly, and worse than
silly. It locks us collectively into a cycle of indulgence
and surprise. Most of the time, there's the fingers-in-
ears denial that anything could ever be wrong, peri-
odically interrupted by stagy astonishment when
something goes so wrong it can't be ignored. We have
to keep numbing ourselves up with nonsense. St
Augustine's 'cruel optimism' rules, cynically abetted by
the sharp minds in the marketing department, who
know that nothing stimulates anxiety and unhappiness
and therefore spending like images of perfection, kept
humiliatingly before us. Christianity says that human
beings are neither perfect nor perfectible. The pre-
sumption of innocence is a useful rule in court cases,
but not a sensible attitude for adults in general to take
to adults in general. In comparison, Christianity says
that both less and more is to be expected of people.
Less because of our inevitably divided and thwarting
selves; more because thanks to grace our identities are
more provisional, more hopefully fluid, than we com-
monly acknowledge. If you're a Christian, you believe
that there's room even in the darkest places, even when

the weight of inevitability seems total, for the sudden and unpredictable and unpredicted leap toward the risk of love.

It is not always clear *how* though, in a given situation, you are supposed to try to be loving. Since Christianity isn't one of the law-religions, it doesn't furnish you with a list of rules. It offers instead the impossible ideal of valuing other people as absolutely as you value yourself, which does not translate straightforwardly into a code of behaviour. (To say the least.) You have the deep patterning in the Christian understanding of the human landscape to guide you; and you have the wisdom embodied in tradition, as well as the prejudices and blindnesses; and you have the history of the earlier attempts made by all your predecessors. But none of these can wholly fix or pin down reliably for you what it is going to mean in everyday terms, this very moment, to love your neighbour as yourself. So you will have to decide, and keep deciding, what you think it means. You will have the freedom – or, to put it another way, the unending responsibility – of working out which way you're supposed to make your imperfect attempt at the impossible task.*

To *love* people. Does that mean you should be trying

---

* If, by the way, this sounds surprisingly like the standard situation of the autonomous modern individual, then what I can say but, duh. And also: no shit, Sherlock. You live in a very, very Christian culture. Christianity's eloquent silences about the means to the Christian end lie behind large portions of modern thinking about liberty.

to give them what they want? Does Jesus's advice about giving away even your clothes mean that your answer should always be yes when someone asks you for help? But what about the times when love requires you not to give the £10 note to the junkie but to deny them the means to their self-destruction? What about the times when love requires you to lock your alcoholic husband out of the house? In that case, you're distinguishing between what people want and what they need; between the cases where love is shown by trusting someone else's desire and where it must be shown by overruling their desire and trying to give them what you judge they ought to have instead. But then who are you to decide? Maybe with a child, the responsibility is plain, no matter how wrong your decisions may turn out to be; but what is to happen when you are only an adult gazing sideways at your fellows? Who says then on which occasions it will be right for you to make presumptuous guesses about their wants and needs, or for them to do the same for you? Or what about forgiveness? When should the mercy we think all receive from God mean that the worldly sanctions for an action should be withheld, and when not? When is it a mercy to someone to let them off a punishment, and when, on the contrary, would it be love's work, mercy's work, to ensure that they are taken seriously enough to suffer their action's penalty? How with your limited knowledge, your pathetically restricted view, can you do more than guess? And then, when is enough love enough? Need is endless, let alone want, and no signal is ever going to come telling you that the world is satisfied now, and you may stop with the job of love done; yet you are finite, and so are your resources of time and emotion, and presumably you are not supposed to immolate yourself, to damage yourself, to let the pile of need bury you. Presumably you must keep back enough of yourself for yourself so that (like the church) you can be there viably tomorrow. But how are you to know when some particular piece of need is one piece too many? It will be just as real, just as urgent, as any of the others, so how will you be able to tell that this time it is permissible to say no? The questions multiply. Accommodating impossibility within the possible world is tricky. As hard as fitting eternity within time, or making a set a member of itself.

My local free paper regularly runs a pair of jousting small ads. Someone pays to put in JESUS IS 4 U, and someone else pays to put in YOU CAN BE GOOD WITHOUT GOD, often next to it. They're talking past each other, though. Because if you're a Christian, what Jesus is for, or maybe 4, is to make the offer of help woven into the fabric of the universe; the one you need when not being good becomes a problem. If you're managing to be good, great. The existence of goodness is not in doubt from the Christian point of view: it's just that we think that you're likely to have to take a turn, in time, at being the puke-stained other brother. And yes, of course you can be 'good without God'. I suppose from a philosophical point of view Christians tend to believe that all successful goodness is a remote reflection of God's. But where motive is concerned, where adherence to a view of the world is concerned, there's obviously no necessary connection at all between belief in God and virtue. The place is stuffed with atheists and agnostics doing devotedly benign things, acting on ideals of compassion and dignity and mutual aid, relieving suffering, working to save or improve the planet.* There are a lot of paths to virtue, mercifully, and absolutely no way there could be a religious or Christian monopoly on it. The point of Christianity is not that it produces virtue. It does, I suppose, have one advantage when it comes to doing good, in that your advance certainty, as a Christian, that you're going to fail at goodness provides a kind of assurance that goodness is worth trying independently of results. It helps a little, therefore, with being good in circumstances where doing good can do no good as far as making progress is concerned. Where things just won't get better, in measurable terms, for all the devotion you pour in. Virtuous and idealistic atheists are at work all over the place, but it is observable that a surprisingly large number of believers are to be found among those who volunteer to work with the dying, the demented, the addicted, the institutionalised and the very impaired and afflicted, where the best that can be done is to love for the sake of it, and to keep sorrow company.

---

* And dying well, too. Witness the Humean courage and dignity of Christopher Hitchens's exit in December 2011.

The same uncertainty applies when you move, as a Christian, from individual behaviour to the question of what you're supposed to hope for as a citizen. To politics, in other words. It is just as disputable how the Christian story should be put into public practice as into private. Again, there is no rulebook telling you how you should get from the general, impossible command to love to its embodiment in anything resembling actual policies. It's a matter for judgement, argument, opinion. Historically, there is no such thing as a single 'Christian' politics, and there couldn't be. In different times and places, different parts of the Christian repertoire come to the fore. To different people, Christianity has seemed to suggest, or endorse, or demand, very different political movements. Christian Socialism in nineteenth-century England and Christian Democracy in post-Second World War Italy and West Germany; fervent religious nationalism in Ireland and Poland and fervent religious imperialism in Russia; Marxism in Central America in the 1980s and self-help small-business ownership in Peru and Brazil in the 2000s; the 'social gospel' of black churches in the US and the vehement right-wing Republicanism of white 'values voters' there. And absolutely all of these are intelligible developments of the gospel. None of them are illegitimate and none of them are compulsory. For again, you are free to decide for yourself. Or required to. Whatever the 'Christian conservatives' in America say, there is no one set of rightful opinions that follow on automatically from your belief. If you have signed

up for the redeeming love of God, you don't – you really
don't – have to sign up too for low taxes, creationism,
gun ownership, the death penalty, closing abortion clin-
ics, climate change denial and grotesque economic in-
equality. You are entirely at liberty to believe that the
kingdom would be better served by social justice, re-
distributive taxation, feminism, gay rights and excellent
public transport. You won't have the authoritative sanction of the gospel for believing in those things either, of
course. But you can. Manifestos can be built on Christianity, but Christianity itself is not a manifesto.

On the other hand, what you can't do, no matter
how tempting, is to push wholly away from you those
who do their Christianity very differently. You can't say:
no kin of mine. I can find Sarah Palin, for example,
as politically ridiculous and terrifying as (perhaps) you
do, but I can't just shun her. No matter how strange,
bizarre and repulsive the expressions of her faith may
be to me, I have to believe that she's got something
right, that she's a member like me of the body of
Christ, in need like me of the grace of God, and as
sure to receive it. She is, despite everything, a sister.
And I have to recognise her as such, while being very
glad that Alaska is a long, long way away; and to hope
that, in the same way, she would recognise a brother in
me, despicable gunless high-taxin' Euro-weenie social-
ist that I am. And the same applies to other alarming
Christians down through history, from Serbian militiamen to Pope Gregory XVI trying to ban railways to
all of the Protestant and Catholic massacre-merchants

of the Wars of Religion. I do not consider myself to be on the hook for their actions, any more than A. C. Grayling should be considered answerable for an atheist monster like Mao. I disagree profoundly with them. But I can't just disavow them. I share like them in the HPtFtU – and in the hope of its remedy. This is not very comfortable. Here Christianity overspills the separate categories by which we conventionally understand the world now, insisting to an awkward degree on common ground.

Also, though you have to make your own mind up about how your religion should influence your politics, you don't have a completely unconstrained choice. Beneath the map of modern opinion, Christianity draws your attention to an older map of experience, which it insists is realler, and takes priority if it comes to a choice. This is the reason why you can find yourself puzzling people by owning a set of perceptions which seem bizarrely jumbled, in terms of current partisan positions, as if you didn't seem able to see the obvious boundary-lines on the modern map. You do see them, of course: it's just that your older map in many places shows 'liberal' and 'conservative' terrain as variants of the same thing, both of them being descended from what was once one theological position. (Think of the way that an American Catholic who holds to traditional Catholic social teaching becomes simultaneously left-wing about the death penalty and right-wing about abortion.) But more importantly, the map of Christian possibilities has edges. There are some forms of politics, therefore, that just aren't open to you as a Christian, because they're off the edge of the older map. They depend on assumptions that are fundamentally incompatible with the Christian essentials, however freely and widely you interpret them.

For example. You can't be a Christian and hold that the ends justify the means. You may not declare it to be a virtue to inflict suffering so that good may come of it: that's flat-out incompatible with the commandment to love, and its inverse, the prohibition on treating people as instruments or conveniences or objects. Of course, you *will* treat people that way, from time to time, the HPtFtU being what it is. You may even have to, like General Montgomery ordering his divisions forward into the minefields. Means–end problems are intrinsic to this world, and can't be dismissed any more than the human need for law can be dismissed. But you may not call the ill you do, or have to do, anything but ill. You may not relabel it as efficiency, or patriotism, or passionate conviction, or being scientific, or being unsentimental, or shaking off the cobwebs of the past. You are to confess it, not build a programme on it. Or take a seemingly opposite (though in fact linked) political temptation. You may not, as a Christian, endorse any politics that dismisses the HPtFtU. You're committed to Jesus's kind pessimism, remember. Pictures of perfection are not for you.* You can believe

---

* 'Pictures of perfection, as you know, make me sick and wicked' – Jane Austen. Quite.

in human betterment to your heart's content, according to whatever policy prescription strikes you as good, but you may not believe, ever, in humanity reaching a state where our wishes are all in mysterious harmony, and our hearts are all conveniently scrubbed and disinfected. It isn't going to happen. So you can be a revolutionary or you can be a reactionary, and that's OK, but you can't, exactly, be a utopian. Except, wait, there's an irony here. The further reason you aren't available for the project of utopia is that you've already got one. What inoculates you against utopia is the hope of the kingdom (of which so many secular utopias are echoes). The kingdom too is a dream impossible to realise in the medium of power; the kingdom too is an impossibility that changes the shape of the possible world by pulling and pulling at us with the promise of a fullness and a kindness beyond our limits, till we discover fullnesses and kindnesses we wouldn't have believed we could manage, had we not set off towards impossibility. How we are to apply this in the world of finite choices and opportunity costs, God leaves as an exercise for the reader.

My own church is spared a lot of the temptations of power, thanks to its ramshackle state. (See the footnote in the previous chapter for a brisk survey of said ramshackle-itude.) There's an assumption among the kind of atheists who think they're engaged in a zero-sum prestige contest with religion, where Superstition™ loses every time Reason™ gains, that we must mind this terribly. That we must be in something resembling the agonised state of the Wicked Witch of the West as the water dissolves us; that we must be shrieking with despondency and humiliation as we lose our grip on our old public standing in England. But I don't think this is really true. There were – still are – some benign aspects of the C. of E.'s established status, like the inclusiveness it implies, the readiness to be there for anyone and everyone who may need it. And I don't, myself, see a problem with having Anglican bishops in the House of Lords, so long as it goes on being a revising chamber rather than an elected senate, especially if they were to be joined *ex officio* by some Catholic bishops, the Chief Rabbi, an imam or two, some Hindu and Buddhist representatives and a selection of secular philosophers. Why *wouldn't* you want the accumulated moral traditions of the country on hand to look at our legislation? On the whole, though, the weight of power is a burden not missed, now that it's gone.

I'm only just old enough myself to remember the way things were before. The world I know, as a Christian, is the one in which we're a small minority. A small minority with an organic link to the symbolism, the buried logic and the dream-life of the wider culture, but still a minority without clout. I know there was another world before this one, in which Christianity was the unconsidered default state of the civilisation, but it was dying when I was a child in the 1960s and 1970s, and it's gone now, and I don't think I would like it back. This way, Christianity is no one's vehicle for ambition. This way, Christianity has been detached from the self-importance of the self-important. This way, it isn't part of the inevitable bullshit of dignitaries any more. This way, the extent to which God is greater than us and any of our stuff – *Allahu akhbar!* – has become helpfully distinct from the inequities of human societies. We're no longer likely to perceive one continuous hierarchy stretching up from the poor to the rich to royalty to God, turning ineffable partway up but forming a single ladder of subordination. This way, the strangeness of Christianity can be visible again. Without the inevitability, without the static of privilege fuzzing the channel, we can pick out again more clearly the counter-cultural call it makes, to admit your lack of cool, and your incompleteness, and your inability ever to be one of the self-possessed creatures in the catalogues, or the loveless calculator that is *Homo economicus*, and to find hope instead; a hope that counts upon, is kindly raised upon, the mess you actually are.

So, no, I don't think that most British Christians are in mourning for times past. And though I wrote this book to try to extricate for people, from the misleading ruins of half-memory, what Christianity feels like from the inside, I don't expect the religion ever to be any less ramshackle, in my time, where I live. And that's all right. For sure, it would be nice if people weren't quite so rude. It would be nice if they didn't brandish crude cartoons of nineteenth-century thought as the very latest thing in philosophy, and expect you to reel back, dazzled. It would be nice not to be patronised by nitwits. It would be nice if people were to understand that science is a special exercise in perceiving the world without metaphor, and that, powerful though it is, it doesn't function as a guide to those very large aspects of experience that can't be perceived *except* through metaphor. It would be nice if people saw that the world cannot be disenchanted, and that the choice before us is really a choice of enchantments.

It would be nice. But it isn't necessary. Because the churches are open, doing their ancient and necessary business, and they will still be open tomorrow, and the day after that, and the day after that, onwards into far time, in some form or other. And it doesn't really matter what form, much though we may love the form they have now. They will still be offering the hush in which we can bear to find out what we're like. Christ will still be looking across at us from the middle of the angry crowd. God will still be there, shining.

If, that is, there is a God. There may well not be. I don't know whether there is. And neither do you, and neither does Richard bloody Dawkins, and neither does anyone. It not being, as mentioned before, a knowable item. What I do know is that, when I am lucky, when I have managed to pay attention, when for once I have hushed my noise for a little while, it can feel as if there is one. And so it makes emotional sense to proceed as if He's there; to dare the conditional. And not timid death-fearing emotional sense, or cowering craven master-seeking sense, or censorious holier-than-thou sense, either. Hopeful sense. Realistic sense. Battered-about-but-still-trying sense. The sense recommended by our awkward sky fairy, who says: don't be careful. Don't be surprised by any human cruelty. But don't be afraid. Far more can be mended than you know.

Notes

I wrote almost the whole of this book sitting at the corner table by the window in the Sidney Street, Cambridge branch of Costa Coffee. I'd like to thank the staff there for their friendliness and tolerance as I nursed my cups of black Americano, hour after hour.

Much of the book repeats things I learned from the three people it is dedicated to. I hope they know how grateful I am that they taught them to me.

For their generous comments on parts of the manuscript, or the whole of it, I am indebted to Bernice Martin, Jenny Turner, Claerwen James, Marina Benjamin, Maura Dooley, Ann Malcolm, Tim Hooper, and the monthly writers' workshop run by my 2007–8 MA students at Goldsmiths College.

I have checked facts and quotations, but I haven't done any research for this book. It is, designedly, just a report from the inside of my head, drawing on what's already in there.

I don't need to point out that I am not any kind of spokesman for the Church of England, do I?

ff

Faber and Faber is one of the great independent publishing houses. We were established in 1929 by Geoffrey Faber with T. S. Eliot as one of our first editors. We are proud to publish award-winning fiction and non-fiction, as well as an unrivalled list of poets and playwrights. Among our list of writers we have five Booker Prize winners and twelve Nobel Laureates, and we continue to seek out the most exciting and innovative writers at work today.

Find out more about our authors and books
faber.co.uk

Read our blog for insight and opinion on books and the arts
thethoughtfox.co.uk

Follow news and conversation
twitter.com/faberbooks

Watch readings and interviews
youtube.com/faberandfaber

Connect with other readers
facebook.com/faberandfaber

Explore our archive
flickr.com/faberandfaber